For my three Sons

and their Families

with undying Love

Are You Going to Heaven?*

Being a "Good Person" . . .

WILL NOT

. . . buy you a ticket to Heaven

Thoughts, Passages and Verses
Collected and Prepared by Grandma Pam

iUniverse, Inc.
Bloomington

Are You Going to Heaven? This question is addressed many times throughout these pages. Relative biblical verses are annotated by an (asterisk)

iUniverse books may be ordered through booksellers or by contacting:

iUniverse
1663 Liberty Drive
Bloomington, IN 47403
www.iuniverse.com
1-800-Authors (1-800-288-4677)

Because of the dynamic nature of the Internet, any Web addresses or links contained in this book may have changed since publication and may no longer be valid.

ISBN: 978-1-4502-5890-6 (sc)
ISBN: 978-1-4502-5891-3 (ebk)

Printed in the United States of America

iUniverse rev. date: 12/27/2010

Preface

Many, many years ago I was born and raised as a citizen of the United States which was established by its forefathers as one nation under God. During the last half of the 20th century I felt helpless watching my country (and many other parts of the world) rapidly changing very drastically.

Somewhere along the way we lost the simple life, we learned to lock our doors against fear, enough was never enough as we selfishly cultivated gluttony and greed and yes, we neglected to send our children to Sunday church school.

Christianity in the United States grew from a faith into ugly "religions" divided and sub-divided into various religious, social and political factors. Unfortunately, only a dedicated minority of Americans today still acknowledge God as the supreme being who blesses our country and oversees the universe.

Because I accept the responsibility for inadequately raising my share of today's generation and therefore contributing to today's world being spiritually deprived, it is my intent to introduce you to my God (and yours) through this bible-based book.

As you read and reread the meanings within, and not just the words, shared insights and wisdom of the Spirit of God will be revealed.

I sincerely hope you enjoy your journey.

Introduction

If you think one day you are going to heaven because you are a Christian, or because you go to church, or you are a good person or maybe you can earn your way by doing good works in this world, I have written this book especially for you. Unfortunately, these actions of "goodness" will not buy you a ticket to heaven.

If, when your time comes, you have time to decide you want to go to heaven (certainly better than an eternity of non-existence or nothingness, or worse yet, the devilish, hellish alternative) you might find this book interesting, informative and worth your time.

If, however, when your time comes you decide you want to go to heaven but never got around to reading this book and making your reservations, you might have run out of time. Simply said, it might then be too late. Unfortunately, you may not only lose out on a heavenly eternal life but you will have missed all the wonders of really "living" life on earth.

For those of you who think heaven is not a "real" place, I am hoping this book will give you something challenging to think about.

I am sure that it is later than you think!

Contents

Book I

Who We Are

Book I

Who We Are

Who are you? Who and what you are is a soul; a soul who lives in a body. We all know that we each live in a physical body until we die at which time our bodies turn to dust. But without our soul the physical body would be just an empty shell. Imagine a world without souls. Imagine a world of empty shells; a world of robots or zombies.

> ### Genesis 2:7 (KJV)
> *And the LORD God formed man of the dust of the ground, and breathed into his nostrils the breath of life; and man became a living soul.*

The soul is the essence of our being. It is who we are. It is what makes us different from anyone else. Because of our heart and mind we are an unique compilation of traits and characteristics that distinguish us from each other.

The universal concept of the soul is eternal and usually believed to preexist the birth of the body. God says that our essence or soul existed with Him in heaven before we were born and our soul will return to heaven and His judgment when our bodies die,

> ### Jeremiah 1:5 (KJV)
> *Before I formed thee in the belly I knew thee; and before thou came forth out of the womb I sanctified thee, and I ordained thee prophet unto the nations*

The soul is so very important because it is an immortal soul: It will not die but lives eternally. Your soul is your self, your being, who you are whether in an earthly body or a spiritual body. And because the word of God (the Holy Bible) is known as food for the soul, I have sprinkled its verses throughout these pages.

> *John 10:28 (ASV)*
> *and I give unto them eternal life; and they shall never perish.*
> *John 11:26 (KJV)*
> *[Jesus speaking to Martha]*
> *And whosoever liveth and believeth in me shall never die....*

The soul is largely the expression of our personality. It is a personality continually developing and influencing our ideas, the situations we think about and how we react. It is composed of intangible characteristics and emotions such as attitudes, motivations, feelings, and behaviors.

Additionally, the soul expresses our will. We have a free will to make choices and decisions. Sure, we all make wrong choices and decisions sometimes which become part of our life experience. Addictions and bad habits are wrong choices. Whenever we hide or sneak doing something, it is a wrong choice.

When it comes to the one paramount choice we must all eventually make (or due to our omission it will be automatically made for us) God wants us all to have the opportunity to freely accept eternal life with Him.

Another primary activity of our soul is the expression of our mind. Our mind is not to be confused with our brain which is part of our physical body. Theories about the mind have been universally debated for centuries with ever

4

changing viewpoints and definitions. Simply explained, the mind uses information learned and stored by the brain. The mind then retains, processes and develops thought patterns and information. It seems reasonable then, that the soul's prosperity and positive wellbeing are a result of an active and productive mind.

Besides the body and soul, all human beings also have a spirit. We are a mind-body-spirit connection. Although separate, the spirit usually stays with or within our souls. Too many people exist without the spirit awakened and functioning within them. It would be similar to a gas tank only two-thirds full which would fuel an adventure with the same power as a full tank. But unfortunately, it couldn't last as long or go as far and would, therefore, miss out on one-third of the adventure.

Even more worrisome are souls who receive negative spirits or evil intercessors. We learn to identify at an early age who among us are a rival, antagonist, the bully, the enemy who (if not guided correctly) in later years develop into a transgressor, crook, outlaw, gangster or evildoer.

We must learn to listen to our (inner) spirit. Traditionally, it has been believed our spirit develops and grows (either positively or negatively) as an essential characteristic of our being. The individual human spirit is, just as is the soul, subject to non-conspicuous changing and growing.

Essentially, it is by our spirit that human beings are able to contact God. When the Holy Spirit of God enters our spirit, we experience complete confidence in life's path. Answers are provided. Obstacles fall away. Miracles happen. And, just as our soul belongs to God immediately upon our physical death, so does our spirit at once return to God.

>*Ecclesiastes 12:7 (ASV)*
>
>*and the dust returneth to the earth as it was, and the spirit returneth unto God who gave it.*

Made in God's image, we are souls who have a spirit. While alive upon earth, we live in a physical body.

>*Genesis 1:27 (KJV)*
>
>*So God created man in his own image, in the image of God created he him; male and female created he them.*
>
>*Psalm 8:5,*
>
>*For thou [Lord] has made him [man] a little lower than the angels and has crowned him with glory and honor.*
>
>*8:6 Thou made him [man] to have dominion over the works of thy hands; Thou has put all things under his feet:*

Our spirit is the manifestation of our intellect. Our spirit is, for instance, that inner voice that warns you to take a different route to work one day and you later learn you thereby avoided a major calamity. Or maybe it was responsible for those misplaced keys appearing on that table you carefully checked only a few minutes before. Or perhaps you had a dream that explained or was a long-awaited answer to a situation. Many accomplished producers especially of but not limited to writings, music and artistic works, recognize they alone (in the natural) are not totally responsible for the magnificence of their works.

Our lives are very fragile,
as is a vapor:
Just a wisp!

Book II

The Trinity

Book II

The Trinity

The Trinity is also frequently referred to as the Godhead. It is the three distinct characteristic aspects of God united into one supernatural almighty power: Three separate entities in one being. Each is totally independent with his own personality and separate role or function.

I think of God the Father as the essence or *soul* of this eternal being. He has the ideas and makes the plans. He is the designer and architect.

Jesus the Son is the *body* of the Trinity through which we are now able to come to God. He is the doer, the generator or achiever who makes sure God's plans are carried out.

The Holy Spirit is the intellect or mind of God revealed to us as he melds with and empowers our being. Primarily, He provides for and guides us in our day-to-day existence. And just as important, He reveals the Holy Bible to us so that we can understand not just its words but its meaning. Of utmost importance, He is with us always.

II Corinthians 13:14
The grace of the Lord Jesus Christ, and the love of God, and the communion [fellowship] of the Holy Ghost [Holy Spirit] be with you all.

Chapter 1

Knowing God

In order to know God, to love Him and to have a relationship with Him you do not need to be religious. Neither do you need to belong to a church nor belong to an organized religion. There is no race or age requirement, physical requirement, intellectual or financial minimum, socially acceptable boundary or any other guideline. There are NO prerequisites.

> **Romans 10:12 (ASV)**
> *For there is no distinction between Jew and Greek: for the same Lord is Lord of all, and is rich unto all that **call** upon him:*
> [I highlighted the word **call** because in this case it means pray to, praise, give thanks in advance, request, etc.]

If you are uncertain or unconvinced that God exists, let's start by acknowledging the possibility that God does *not* exist. If it is possible that God does *not* exist, then the opposite is also possible. It is therefore, possible that God *does* exist. Now, I acknowledge that there is no amount of evidence that can prove to your satisfaction that God exists. But neither is there any amount of evidence that can prove to your satisfaction that God does not exist.

Yes I know, just because something is possible, doesn't mean it is a reality. It has often been argued that it is impossible to either prove or disprove the existence of God. In any case, we can only discuss possibilities until something is "proven" to us personally. I may not believe something you know to be true and "proven" to your satisfaction to be true until it is also "proven" to my satisfaction. If we keep ourselves open to any and all possibilities, in His time, God will prove Himself to you.

Many people are struggling with the idea of the existence of God. Usually unbelief is simply due to lack of knowledge. Disbelief, however, is the result of our doubt, refusal or inability to accept knowledge. Refusing Him once you gain knowledge is disobedience. Christians are taught that God saves us from sin and corruption. If however we reject Him, we become corrupted by sin which makes us both unworthy of God and the eternal life He offers. God tells us in the book of Romans that if we refuse to turn to Him because of our stubbornness, we are making things more difficult for ourselves. Unfortunately, we will not have any recourse on judgment day when we will experience His fair accounting and His anger.

Perhaps the greatest evidence worldwide that God exists is believers, whose lives (and hearts) are changed by the grace of God. The existence of God (and Christianity) requires a leap of faith. We will not know the presence of God unless we seek him.

Throughout history it has been proposed that "If God did not exist, we would probably create Him." Human beings seem to need the possibility of a supreme being. Deep within the human heart is a sense that there must be something more, something powerful, something immortal about our life.

I would like to introduce you to Blaise Pascal. Although many of you will recognize his name, I have included a very brief overview of his significance as well as a couple of his renown ideas.

> Blaise Pascal (1623-1662), a very influential mathematician, physicist and philosopher was a child prodigy who was considered one of the great minds of the Western World.
>
> His logical thinking skills resulted in numerous and significant contributions in several areas of mathematics and science as well as literature and religion.

Pascal identified a deep spiritual void in the lives of all mankind; a void that only the Lord himself is able to fill. Publicly he declared it a "God-shaped vacuum in every man." In addition, entitling it Pascal's Wager, the great French philosopher made the following observation:

> "If God *does not* exist, and you don't believe in Him, you've not lost anything. If God *does* exist and you don't believe in Him, you've lost everything."

Which, of course, also means if God does not exist, and you believe in Him, you've not lost anything. And if God does exist, and you believe in Him, you've gained everything. Pascal logically summed up that it is a better wager to believe in God than not to do so.

Thus, I have everything to gain and nothing to lose by believing in God, and I have everything to lose and nothing to gain by not believing in God. Now, I may be an old lady, but I don't need to be hit over the head to understand which is the more intelligent choice.

If we have acknowledged our belief in God or at least the possibility he may exist, then shouldn't we derive some benefit from knowing him or at least knowing about him. It seems to me that any God wouldn't be small or insignificant but probably immense with God-sized capabilities and God-sized powers. Envision a supreme, supernaturally powerful being over the entire universe who is immortal. He is the Creator. He is the eternal Father. He is the Source of the universe and everything within including our physical and spiritual lives.

Psalm 29:4 (KJV)

The voice of the LORD is powerful; the voice of the LORD is full of majesty.

As believers, God immediately gives us love, joy and peace. These fabulous gifts are better described as unequaled love, joy beyond description and an indescribable inner peace. Unfortunately, their impact cannot be explained but can only be experienced.

Yes, these are great gifts, but if God is really God, and God is all powerful, then why not hope for a miracle or a physical healing or something big. Absolutely, it doesn't hurt to shoot for the moon. But for most of us, we will have to learn to fly before we can take off the first time in an airplane.

The next logical step is to have hope (for something), and then have faith that it will be. Belief requires faith, which requires hope. We learn to have faith in God by "acting" as if we believe. We are, in effect, changing our attitude, rather than our reasoning.

Accept Him by saying "God I trust you...it's not up to me to figure it out." Receive the impossible by believing (for) the unbelievable. To know God is to believe in Him.

Hebrews 11:6 (KJV)

But without faith it is impossible to please him: for he that cometh to God must believe that he is, and that he is a rewarder of them that diligently seek him

I recently watched a television replay of one of Billy Graham's Canadian crusades from the late 1960s where he was talking about the apostle Paul's epistle to the Corinthians. As Rev. Graham pointed out, Paul makes it clear in his writings that we cannot come to God by wisdom, but we must come by faith.

True faith, and thereby belief, comes by hearing the word of God. Since the Holy Bible is often referred to as 'The Word' of God, it seems reasonable that faith comes from hearing (or reading) the Bible. But I am convinced that God's voice is broader and less limited than our earthly comprehensions. In the following instance at least, the word of God must include the will of God which is not only expressed in the Bible but through all His communications.

Romans 10:17 (KJV)

So then faith [belief] cometh by hearing, and hearing by the word of God

God loves us because of who God is, not because of anything we did or didn't do. Most of us are aware of the existence of different kinds of love. God is pure, enduring love. Love which is patient and kind. Love is His nature. True, we cannot measure love because it has no physical properties. Love is difficult for most of us to adequately describe. Like the wind, we cannot see it but we can recognize its' effects and results.

Exodus 34:6 (KJV)
..The LORD God, merciful and gracious longsuffering [slow to anger], and abundant in goodness [loving kindness] and truth,

God is faithful (to His Word) and compassionate. He never changes. Although God is all powerful, He never does anything to us but only does things for us. We never need to be fearful because God loves us and will take care of us. He wants to fill us with his gifts, knowledge and wisdom.

Isaiah 40:8
The grass withers, the flower fades: but the word of our God shall stand for ever.

Hebrews 13:8 (NLT)
Jesus Christ is the same yesterday, today and for ever.

Revelation 1:8
I am the Alpha and the Omega [the beginning and the ending] says the Lord God. I am the Almighty One who is, who always was and who is yet to come.

*Titus 2:11 (NIV)
For the grace of God that brings salvation has appeared to all men [people].

Grace is the power of God, freely given to us who believe. Each day we are given a new portion of grace. God has given us a portion of faith...use it.

The Lord's love is with those who fear (obey, revere) Him. I believe when we put God first in every *thing* we do, He puts us first in every *thing* He does. To love God is the first Commandment.

> ****Matthew 22:37 (KJV)***
>
> *Jesus said unto him, Thou shalt love the Lord thy God with all thy heart, and with all thy soul, and with all thy mind.*
>
> ***John 15:12 (KJV)***
>
> *This is my commandment, That ye love one another, as I have loved you.*

Before I met God, I foolishly believed that the universe provided for our needs. Sure, anyone I said that to thought I was crazy. But I realized my needs were always somehow met. Maybe not to my liking or my choice. But the basics were provided and I somehow survived through the tough times.

God speaks through circumstances. I know of people who always like to claim the glory but the glory belongs to God. The Lord Will Provide. If God ensures the birds in the air have enough to eat, we should trust God will care for us. Never question (doubt) Him. Don't be anxious. Don't worry or fear (the opposite of faith): Worry causes destructive, negative results. Never worry about "stuff." You can't take it with you.

> ***Matthew 6:25 (NLT)***
>
> *That is why I tell you not to worry about everyday life—whether you have*

enough food and drink, or enough clothes to wear. Isn't life more than food, and your body more than cloth-ing?

Let God transform you into a new person by changing the way you think. Then you will learn to know God's will for you, which is good and pleasing and perfect.

James 1:17

Every good and perfect gift is from above, coming down from the Father of the heavenly lights, who does not change like shifting shadows.

God is a living God! He is God to living human beings. He is God to living souls. He is himself a living soul. He is not God to the dead who are sleeping. He wants a relationship with us. He wants a deep and everlasting relationship and the best way to start and maintain a relationship is through prayer.

Prayers and Vows

Jeremiah 33:3 (KJV)
Call unto me, and I will answer thee, and show thee great and mighty things which thou knowest not.

Prayer is simply talking with God. It's so simple yet so very, very powerful. God wants us to talk with Him about everything; about all our cares all the time. Not just on Sunday mornings or once a day but all day long. He wants to become an active part of our lives. We can talk to God anytime. We can pray anywhere. Prayer is not restricted to being on our knees, at the bedside or the dinner table.

We can pray while driving (with our eyes open, please). We can pray out loud or silently (because He hears our hearts). Eventually, it will become natural to talk with Him often throughout the day as situations arise. He is always there for us. Yes, God knows our needs and situations but He can only respond directly to our prayers, our requests. It is up to us to keep the door open. Pray boldly! The Lord delights in us fearlessly coming into His presence, and He will bless us in miraculous ways.

Although God is touched by our needs, tears and pain, He is *moved* by our faith (trust). Prayer can change circumstances in our lives. But if you want God to give to you, then give to Him first. Give of your time, give praise, give thanks, give a kind word or a helping hand and give to others. Trust in His power and His mercy and expect to receive.

God works in His own time frame. Sometimes prayers are answered immediately but often they are answered in the framework of the bigger picture which usually involves other people and situations. And although He always answers our prayers, sometimes the answer is no! Talk *to* your problem but don't talk about it. Speak as if it is already solved or cured or at least in the process. In God's universe we have to believe before we see. I believe it, therefore it will happen. Believe 'n pray -- believe 'n receive.

If you have to see it to believe it,
you won't believe it when you see it.

Jesus proclaimed that the Lord's Prayer is an example of how we are to pray. It begins (and in this case also ends) with acknowledgment and praise of Our Father. It puts God first. It then says we are here to continue on our daily enlightened journey which requires sustenance and guidance. We are to ask His forgiveness (the importance of forgiving will be discussed in another section). Additionally, we pray for his protection and safekeeping. Again, it offers praise and glory. So Be It. (Amen).

Matthew 6:9, (KJV)
...Our Father which art in heaven,
Hallowed be thy name
6:10 Thy kingdom come, Thy will be done in earth, as it is in heaven.
6:11 Give us this day our daily bread.
6:12 And forgive us our debts, as we forgive our debtors.
6:13 And lead us not into temptation, but deliver us from evil:

For thine is the kingdom, and the power,
and the glory, for ever. Amen.

My personal adaptation of The Lord's Prayer is to first praise God since He delights in our praise and wants us to keep Him first in our thoughts always. Then I thank Him specifically for blessings and answered prayers. Of course, I ask God's forgiveness for my recent daily screw ups. Lastly, I may request a specific blessing, help and/or a healing for others or myself.

Developing any relationship requires some time and commitment. In the beginning I needed to make room in my life for God; for talking with God. As an example, I now find I cannot have a successful day unless I set aside the first part of each day for talking with Him. And I know being first in all things pleases God. Therefore I pray my version of The Lord's Prayer in the early mornings. Of course, each day it is a little different; either a little longer or shorter and scattered throughout is plenty of quiet time when I just listen. It is important to listen carefully because prayer is a two-way street. Listening opens up a two-way communication which is an opportunity for me to receive thoughts, ideas and answers.

Although I sometimes have lengthy prayers at nighttime, I'm learning to talk to God more and more throughout the day. When unexpected events occur in my favor, I praise the Lord right then and there for His mercy and grace. The more often I acknowledge and praise Him, the more favor He bestows upon me. Praising Him releases His powers. I try to make God a part of the minute-by-minute workings of my life. Whether I'm communicating silently or out loud, my goal is to keep Him first.

God speaks to us in many ways which we soon learn to recognize. God speaks to *everybody* who listens. He speaks through His word the Holy Bible, through pastors, through other people, even the radio or television or through that tiny voice inside of us. He speaks through everyday life in many unusual ways. We learn to differentiate between our own ideas and God's will. The more time we spend with God, the more information He will reveal to us.

John 10:27

My sheep [those who specifically hear a revelation from God] hear my voice, and I know them, and they follow me:

I've discovered that God even sometimes talks in an audible voice. One Sunday evening as I stood staring into the darkness from my bedroom window, I cried out in anguish and frustration "Oh God, help me." I wasn't talking to God. I wasn't even thinking about God. I was in an agonizing dilemma about the following day's decisions and activities.

From behind my right shoulder I heard a clear and distinct, powerful yet mellow baritone voice. Startled, I spun around but saw no one, of course, because I knew I was alone in the house. This voice said only "be not concerned, for it is resolved."

Now, I'm not some sort of nut. And I don't ever before remember hearing voices; at least while being sober. Neither had I been to church or said a prayer in probably thirty five years. But somehow I knew that I knew, that I knew in the deepest part inside of me, that this was the voice of God. I tried to sanely and logically review and consider what had just happened.

Deuteronomy 4:36 (KJV)
Out of heaven he made thee to hear his
voice, that he might instruct thee:

Now, I did (in reality) hear the voice. It was not a voice I recognized. It was an extremely pleasant yet powerful voice. The sentence structure was not like my way of speaking so I decided immediately to write down the words so I wouldn't forget them. For example, instead of "be not concerned, for it is resolved," I would have mumbled something like "don't worry, It's taken care of." I remember thinking at the time that the wording was not only eloquent but minimalistic.

Equally impressive was the colossal peace I felt wash over me. Perhaps I have felt almost that peaceful once or twice before in my lifetime. It was something akin to a million pounds of dread being lifted off my heart. When only minutes before I was unable to concentrate on a television program because of the great anguish I was experiencing, I then felt great peace and joy. I couldn't even be concerned when I *tried* to think about my problem situation. I knew in my heart that all was well.

That is true peace -- not an escape from the pressures and trials of life but the quiet repose of a heart at rest with God. Jesus said, "These things I have spoken unto you, that in me ye might have peace."

I remember thinking "wow"...so there really is a God. He must have spoken to me audibly because he knew I was going to be difficult to convince. I have to see everything for myself in black and white and I want things proven to me over and over before I'll even consider their possibility. (I know, but it's an annoying family trait.) By the way, I found out the next morning that the agonizing dilemma I suffered that memorable Sunday evening was resolved as if it evaporated into thin air. Yes, my God performs magic.

For the next several weeks I periodically questioned myself. Could I really have experienced what I believed to be true. But then I remembered the voice and I knew that I knew that deep down in the deepest part of me that it really did happen and it was not my imagination. Besides, I had that slip of paper with the audible words written on it!

Whether or not it happened in my bedroom or in my head is immaterial because at the time I believed deep, deep down inside of me that it was happening, that it was really truly happening. Therefore, at some level, it did happen. And if I didn't want to admit I was "loony," I was compelled to stay with my belief. After a few months, or maybe a few more, I no longer questioned anything.

> **Psalm 18:6, also II Samuel 22:7 (KJV)**
> *In my distress I called upon the LORD, and cried to my God: he heard my voice from his temple [heavenly dwelling place], and my cry came before him, and entered into his ears.*

If you remember nothing else I have written here, please forever remember this one truth:

> If you should find yourself in a dangerous or emergency situation such as amidst a natural disaster, a potential automobile collision or a frightening, life-threatening personal confrontation, and you call out to God for his help (even if silently) he will guide you through your ordeal.

It was in the spring of 2001 when this journey of mine began. I really didn't know where to go next but I thought I might try reading the bible. I located an old King James version which I didn't understand so I soon gave that up. I had to start at a more basic level so I started listening to some of the television evangelists and pastors, at first weekly and then almost daily, learning all I could.

Matthew 13:13 (KJV)

Therefore speak I to them in parables: because they seeing, see not; and hearing they hear not, neither do they understand

Because many daily television programs were available anytime on the computer, it became my bridge to worldwide communications and interactive programs. I also read every faith-based website and blog I could find, including a few which provided the bible verses. So I tried once again to read it because it was not only available in more than fifty languages but was offered in modern everyday language. Also, I heard that beginners like me should start reading with the Book of John (the fourth book in the New Testament). With my failing, aging eyesight the real bonus was the large type-size available on my computer!

Perhaps it was in 2006 or 2007 that I first heard about the movie *Conversations with God*. It was produced after the best-selling book by the same name was written by Neale Donald Walsch. When I Googled Neale Walsch on the computer I found a transcript of a previous interview he did with Larry King on Fox television. Later I watched another interview with Larry King or perhaps it was a re-run. No matter, because I eventually saw the film and my conviction was reconfirmed that our experiences with

God were strikingly similar. It somehow felt reassuring to know I wasn't unique in my experience which offered me encouragement to continue my walk.

And then there is the story about Saul, later renamed Paul:

Acts 9:1, (KJV)

And Saul, yet breathing out threatenings and slaughter [murderous desire] against the disciples of the Lord, went unto the high priest,

9:2 And desired [requested] of him letters to Damascus to the synagogues, [authorizing him] that if he found any of this way [the Way of Jesus Christ], whether they were men or women, he might bring them bound [with chains] unto Jerusalem.

9:3 And as he journeyed, he came near Damascus: and suddenly there shined round about him a light from heaven:

9:4 And he fell to the earth, and heard a voice saying unto him, Saul, Saul, why persecuting [harassing, troubling] thou me?

9:5 And he [Saul] said, Who art thou, Lord? And the Lord said, I am Jesus whom thou are persecuting: it is hard [dangerous and it will turn out badly] for thee to kick against the pricks [to offer vain and perilous resistance].

9:6 And he trembling and astonished said, Lord, what wilt thou have [de-

sire] me to do? And the Lord said unto him, Arise, and go into the city, and it shall be told thee what thou must do.

9:7 And the men, which journeyed with him stood speechless, [in terror], hearing a voice, but seeing no man.

9:8 And Saul arose from the earth; and when his eyes were opened, he saw no man [could see nothing]: but they led him by the hand, and brought him into Damascus.

9:9 And he was three days without sight, and neither did eat nor drink [anything].

Most of us pray to God to ask for something. Often it is because we need or want something which usually means a change for the good in our circumstances. God doesn't always want to give us that fish which will feed us. He wants to teach us to fish so we can feed ourselves. He wants to change us from within and thereby change our lives which will indirectly result in changing our circumstances.

Matthew 18:19, (KJV)

Again I say unto you, That if two of you shall agree on earth as touching anything that they shall ask, it shall be done for them of my Father who is in heaven.

18:20 For where two or three are gathered together in my name, there am I in the midst of them.

In the book of Numbers, Chapter 30, concerning vows, Moses describes the regulations given him by the Lord. Vows are similar to prayers but much more directed. If you want something or need something in desperation, it may be time for a vow. First, you ask God for something and then promise Him something in return.

Numbers 30:2 (NIV)

When a man makes a vow to the LORD or takes an oath to obligate himself by a pledge, he must not break his word but must do everything he said.

Leviticus 23:38 (NIV)

These offerings are in addition to those for the LORD'S Sabbaths and in addition to your gifts and whatever you have and all the freewill offerings you give to the LORD.

God may not answer all your prayers if they are to your detriment or not in accordance with his plans. But God will accept your vows. Just remember there are regulations attached. Basically you *must* uphold your end of the vow on time. Yes, pay up and on time.

Job 22:27 (NIV)

You will pray to him, and he will hear you, and you will fulfill your vow.

Ecclesiastes 5:4, (NIV)

When you make a vow to God, do not delay in fulfilling it. He has no pleasure in fools; fulfill your vow.

5:5 It is better not to vow than to make a vow and not fulfill it.

When we "give" to God, we bring our **self** into wholeness and wellness. We learn to believe by casting our cares onto God and watching Him work in our behalf.

Psalm 61:8(KJV)

So will I sing praise unto thy name for ever, that I may daily perform my vows

Although prayers are usually addressed to God, some prayers are addressed to God in the name of Jesus Christ. There may be times it is important for us to communicate with God silently, i.e. secretly. God hears our heart, He searches and tests our heart, then judges our heart. If you want your prayers answered, be an answer to someone's prayer.

Forgiveness

In God's eyes we are not perfect and pure beings because every person has sinned. Whether we have told a lie or committed a major criminal act, a sin is a sin. Sins don't come in large or small sizes. All must be forgiven before we are worthy to be in God's presence.

Ephesians 4:28 (ASV)

Let him that stole steal no more: but rather let him labor, working with his hands the thing that is good [doing something useful], that he may have whereof to give [something to share] to him that has need.

4:29 Let no corrupt speech [unwholesome talk] proceed out of your mouth, but only what is good for edifying [helpful for building others up] as their need may be, that it may give grace to [benefit] them that hear.

4:30 And grieve not the Holy Spirit of God, in whom you were sealed [marked, branded as God's own, secured] unto the day of redemption [of final deliverance].

4:31 Let all bitterness, and wrath [rage], and anger, and clamor [brawling], and railing [slander], be put away from you [banished], with all malice:

4:32 and be ye kind one to another, tenderhearted [compassionate], forgiving each other, even as God also in Christ forgave you.

I especially like the metaphor of God using his 'heavenly eraser' to remove all trace of our blemished past. The book of Isaiah, Chapter 1, verse 18 declares that although our sins are as scarlet, once forgiven they are as white as snow. And in the book of Psalm, Chapter 103 verse 12 says, "As far as the east is from the west so far hath He removed our transgressions from us." When our sins are forgiven, they are *forgotten*. God repeats His promise to us in the book of Hebrews.

Hebrews 10:17 (ASV)

And their sins and their iniquities will I remember no more.

When God erases our sins, our past is totally clean. Every instance of past errors and failures is erased on our page in God's Book of Life. Never again will they be found recorded among our acts in those heavenly pages. We begin a new life with a clean slate. When one day heaven welcomes us, it will be by God's mercy and not by our good works.

In the words of Billy Graham,
"We are going to heaven by the grace and mercy of god..."

Since we are only human, it is realistic to believe that we will continue to err. That is why we need to continually ask his forgiveness. We not only want to ask His forgiveness because we love Him so wholly, but it is vital to ask God to forgive us for our sins. His forgiveness allows us to eventually be pure in His presence in heaven. We must repent and surrender to Christ. We must trust in the Lord and receive Him by faith alone. Sometimes this is referred to as being born again.

> **II Corinthians 5:17 (KJV)**
> *Therefore if any man be in Christ, he is a new creature: old things are passed away; behold all things are become new.*

Almost immediately we may feel differently. Many have described it as feeling as though they have received a new heart. Over time our attitudes and feelings begin to slowly change. Day-to-day behaviors and thoughts that once seemed normal to us may now seem inappropriate.

The spirit of God comes to live within us and the laws of God are written in our hearts. Our love for Him grows and grows and we want to do what is right because we are overcome by His love for us and how we have become righteous in God's eye. Where does this love come from? God not only feels love, but He is love.

> **Ephesians 3:17 (KJV)**
> *That Christ may dwell [settle down, abide or make His permanent home] in your hearts by faith; that ye, being rooted [deeply] and grounded [securely]in love,*
> *** Mark 16:16**
> *He that believes [who adheres to and trusts in and relies on the Gospel and Him] and is baptized shall be saved [from the penalty of eternal death]; but he who believes not [who does not adhere to and trust in and rely on the Gospel and Him] shall be condemned.*

Our heavenly Father will welcome each of us individually as one of His children and begin a relationship with us. How deep, how meaningful and how productive our new relationship will be will depend upon us. Both the frequency and amount of time spent with God are directly proportional to individual results. Obviously, more equals better.

Salvation is through faith (belief without proof), by grace (God's goodness) and not of our good works. It is a gift of God. God must have designed it that way not only to receive our thanks and praise but also as a method to ensure no one would be able to brag that their being saved is a result of their own doing. Being saved is referred to as salvation because it is free to all.

Ephesians 2:8, (KJV)

For by grace are ye saved through faith; and that not of yourselves: it is the gift of God:

2:9 Not of works, lest any man should boast.

We are directed in Colossians 3:2 to set our affection on things above, not on things of the earth. "Stuff" won't give us true happiness and we certainly can't take it with us in the end. We are directed to make our relationship with God the central issue in our life. We are to desire to know Him (not just about him), fellowship with Him, and live for His glory more than anything else.

There is a saying, "many are called but few are chosen." Depending upon how faithful we are, God anoints the chosen few by invitation. The anointing is the power of God functioning in our daily lives. It changes our thoughts and actions. We change how we spend money, who our friends are and how we dress. It affects what, how much and how often eat, how we talk and what we talk about and even the books, movies and television we enjoy. It affects everything about our earthly living but principally our goals and direction.

The first chapter of First Peter tells how God knew and chose us long ago and that his Spirit made us holy. We have obeyed him and been purified through Christ. God will continue to give us more and more grace and peace.

II Timothy 2:10

I am willing to endure all things that they [those God has chosen] may obtain the salvation with eternal glory which is in Christ Jesus.

* I Peter 5:10 (ASV)

And the God of all grace [who gives all blessing and favor], who called you unto [to share in] his eternal glory [that will continue forever] in Christ Jesus, after you have suffered a little while, shall himself [make you] perfect, establish [keep you from falling, ground you securely], strengthen [and settle] you.

I Timothy 1:17 (KJV)

Now unto the King eternal, immortal, invisible, the only God, be honor and glory forever and ever. Amen.

Promises and Beatitudes

It is said the Bible contains more than 1500 different promises from God. In Isaiah 1:19 we are told that if we are agreeable, willing and obey we will be blessed by consuming the finest the land provides. Examples of God's promises are:

His promise for Health
James 5:15
And the prayer of faith shall save the sick, and the Lord shall raise him up; and if he have committed sins, they shall be forgiven him.

His promise for Deliverance
Psalm 34:7
The Angel of the Lord encamps around those who fear [revere] Him, and He delivers them.

His promise for Finances
Philippians 4:19
My God shall supply all your needs according to His riches in glory by Christ Jesus.

His promise for Assurance
I John 5:14
And this is the confidence that we have in him, that if we ask anything according to his will, he hears us:

One day, in order to deliver a sermon to the multitudes, Jesus ascended a mountain near Galilee with his disciples. Referred to today as the Sermon on the Mount, He taught the difference between *good* and *evil*.

Most importantly, He taught of thriving in the *good* which bestows supreme happiness and blessedness both in this world and the next. Listed here are the first ten key points of His sermon, commonly referred to as the Beatitudes.

Matthew 5:3, (KJV)
Blessed are the poor in spirit: for theirs is the kingdom of heaven.

5:4 Blessed are they that mourn: for they shall be comforted.

5:5 Blessed are the meek: for they shall inherit the earth.

5:6 Blessed are they which do hunger and thirst after righteousness: for they shall be filled.

5:7 Blessed are the merciful: for they shall obtain mercy.

5:8 Blessed are the pure in heart: for they shall see God.

5:9 Blessed are the peacemakers: for they shall be called the children of God.

5:10 Blessed are they which are per-secuted for righteousness' sake: for theirs is the kingdom of heaven.

5:11 Blessed are ye, when men shall revile you, and persecute you, and shall say all manner of evil against you falsely, for my sake.

5:12 Rejoice, and be exceeding glad: for great is your reward in heaven: for so persecuted they the prophets which were before you.

Chapter 2

Knowing Jesus

Philippians 2:9, (ASV)
Wherefore also God highly exalted him, and gave unto him the name which is above every name;
2:10 *that in the name of Jesus every knee should bow, of things in heaven and things on earth and things under the earth,*
2:11 *and that every tongue should confess that Jesus Christ is Lord, to the glory of God the Father.*
Acts 17:3 (ASV)
...this Jesus, whom I proclaim [preach] unto you, is the Christ [the Messiah].

Jesus from Nazareth of Galilee, who is called Christ or The Christ, is referred to as the Son of God, the Son of Man, the Messiah, the Nazarene, the Lamb of God, the Anointed One, the Chosen One, the same as the Father, the Word or the Living Word, Rabbi (teacher), King of Israel, King of the Jews, or King of Kings.

He has also been referred to as the worker of miracles, the healer and/or physician, an exorcist, a prophet, an orator, a preacher, the (good) shepherd and a carpenter.

That Jesus was born and lived more than two thousand years ago is a fairly well-documented historical fact questioned by few. His significance arose from his unique lifestyle and his command of life events. He proclaimed himself to be the Son of God, which is sometimes referred to as the second aspect of the Trinity.

Perhaps as early as one thousand years before Christ's birth, the Hebrew bible (originally written in Hebrew and Aramaic) was documented from oral tradition into written form. The dead sea scrolls and other archaeological finds are written records of early historical works. Several hundred documents from the Hebrew Bible are of great religious and historical significance.

In later centuries from about 150 BC, many manuscripts and disquisitions having mass popular appeal were written by scholars, priests and others. After the birth and death of Christ, the finest or most popular books were selected and preserved. However, instead of creating an anthology, these books (originally written in Greek) were added to the existing Bible. Today, the two sections are clearly separated into the Old Testament and the New Testament which together make up the Christian Holy Bible.

Early Christian literature which claimed to relate in detail the life and teachings of Jesus or divulge the nature of God were called gospels. Today, four accepted gospels have been preserved for common usage. These are the first four books of the New Testament (the gospels of the saints: Matthew, Mark, Luke and John) which tell of the life of Jesus from different perspectives. Although the first three are but slightly different tellings of primarily the same story, the book of John reveals the manifestation of God's eternal word into the flesh as the eminent Jesus who is our Christ. It is often recommended that first-time readers begin studying the Bible with this book of St. John.

In each of the books of Matthew and Luke, we are told that Jesus was born to the virgin Mary in the town of Bethlehem in Judea. This miracle of the Holy Spirit is disclosed in the book of Luke when the angel Gabriel visits Mary to reveal that she has been chosen by God to bear His Son.

Matthew 1:23 (ASV)

Behold, the virgin shall be with child and shall bring forth a son, And they shall call his name Immanuel which is interpreted as God with us.

Again, an angel appears. This time to announce Jesus' birth to shepherds who leave their flocks to honor the newborn babe. Even without telephones, television and the internet word spreads throughout the land.

John 5:23 (ASV)

that all may honor the Son, even as they honor the Father. He that honors not the Son honors not the Father that sent him.

*I John 4:15 (NIV)

If anyone acknowledges that Jesus is the Son of God, God lives in him and he in God.

Before Jesus was even two years old, He was visited by Magi from the east (probably Iraq or Iran) bearing regal gifts. They had been led by a star to worship the Christ who was born King of the Jews. These magi were educated men of means very likely who believed the prophecies about the Messiah in the Old Testament of the Bible.

Matthew 2:1, (KJV)

[description of the visit of the Magi]
Now when Jesus was born in Bethlehem of Judaea in the days of Herod the king, behold, there came wise men from the east to Jerusalem,

2:2 Saying, Where is he that is born King of the Jews? for we have seen his star in the east, and are come to worship him.

2:3 When Herod the king had heard these things, he was troubled, and all Jerusalem with him.

2:4 And when he had gathered all the chief priests and scribes of the people together, he demanded of them where Christ should be born.

2:5 And they said unto him, In Bethlehem of Judaea: for thus it is written by the prophet,

2:6 And thou Bethlehem in the land of Judea, art not the least among the princes of Judea: for out of thee shall come a Governor that shall rule my people Israel.

2:7 Then Herod, when he had privily called the wise men, enquired of them diligently what time the star appeared.

2:8 And he sent them to Bethlehem, and said, Go and search diligently for the young child and when ye have found him, bring me word again, that I may come and worship him also.

2:9 When they had heard the king, they departed; and, lo, the star, which they saw in the east, went before them, till it came and stood over where the young child was.

2:10 When they saw the star, they re-joiced with exceeding great joy.

2:11 And when they were come into the house, they saw the young child with Mary his mother, and fell down, and worshiped him: and when they had opened their treasures, they presented unto him gifts; gold, and frankincense and myrrh.

2:12 And being warned of God in a dream that they should not return to Herod, they departed to their own country another way.

A fearful and threatened King Herod heard of the birth of Jesus and tried to kill Him by massacring all the male children in Bethlehem under the age of two. Because of this action (historically recorded as the "massacre of the innocents") the family fled to Egypt. After Herod's death the family returned and settled in Nazareth.

Acts 13:23

"And it is Jesus, one of King David's descendants, who is God's promised Savior of Israel!

When prophecies of the coming messiah in the old Hebrew Bible where fulfilled, they were written about in Matthew and other Gospels. Such is the case with Jesus' birth, life, death and resurrection. The Gospels of Mathew and Luke both trace the lineage of Jesus from King David and from Abraham before him. Through his mother Mary, Jesus was born to both royal (through Solomon) and priestly (through Levi) genealogy.

This Son of God is also known as God the Son.

The Son

Hebrews 1:5

[The Son Is Greater Than the Angels] For to which of the angels did God ever say what he said to Jesus, "You are my Son. Today I have become your Father." God also said, "I will be a father to him, and he will be a son to me."

John 8:23

... he [Jesus] said unto them, You are from beneath; I am from above. You are of this world; I am not of this world.

John 8:42

Jesus said unto them, If God were your Father, you would love me: for I came forth and have come from God; for I have not come on my own but He sent me

John 12:26 (ASV)

If any man serve me, let him follow me; and where I am, there shall also my servant be: if any man serve me, him will the Father honor.

The existence of Jesus is accepted by a great majority of biblical scholars and historians who describe Him as a healer who preached about God, our heavenly father, and His kingdom. In the gospels of Matthew and Luke, Jesus also speaks about morality, prayer and unconditional self-sacrificing for God and for all people. In John we learn more about Him personally and His divinity.

> ### John 12:44,
> *Jesus declared loudly, The one who believes in Me does not believe in [and trust in and rely on] Me only, but in believing in Me, he believes in Him Who sent Me.*
>
> *12:45 Whosoever sees me, also sees Him who sent me.*
>
> *12:46 I have come into the world as a Light, so that whosoever believes in [trusts in and relies on] Me will not stay in darkness.*

Again and again Jesus proclaims that God the Father in heaven (spirit form) and He on earth (in bodily form) are two aspects of the same being.

> ### John 5:19
> *Jesus answered them saying, I most solemnly assure you, the Son is able to do nothing of His own accord; He is only able to do what He sees the Father doing for whatever the Father does, the Son does in a like manner.*
>
> ### John 12:49, (NIV)
> *For I did not speak of my own accord but the Father who sent me commanded me what to say and how to say it.*
>
> *12:50 I know that his command leads to eternal life. So whatever I say is just what My Father has told Me to say.*

Historians accept that Jesus was baptized by John the Baptist when he was about thirty years of age. John, son of Elisabeth who was a cousin of Jesus' mother Mary, was about six months older than Jesus. Historians are almost unanimous in recognizing Jesus' baptism as a major historical event signifying the beginning of His public ministry.

Luke 1:36 (KJV)

And, behold, thy cousin Elisabeth, she hath also conceived a son in her old age: and this is the sixth month with her, who was called barren.

Recorded accounts proclaimed by the Apostle Mark, describe how Jesus came to (the fork in) the Jordan River where John the Baptist had been preaching and baptizing. John had amassed his usual attentive crowd who became uncertain after Jesus was baptized (as told in the first Chapter of Mark.)

Luke 3:21, (NLT)

One day when the crowds were being baptized, Jesus himself was baptized. As he was praying, the heavens opened, and the Holy Spirit, in bodily form, descended on him like a dove.

3:22 And a voice from heaven said, "You are my dearly loved Son, and you bring me great joy.

The Anointed One

Acts 10:38

God anointed Jesus of Nazareth with the Holy Spirit and with power; and Jesus went around doing good and healing all who were oppressed by the devil, because God was with him.

Jesus made a point of welcoming all walks of life. He was just as likely to speak kindly to women and children, the poor, foreigners and criminals as he was the elite.

John 15:12 (NLT)

This is my commandment: Love each other in the same way I have loved you.

In order to reach the masses both in his day and beyond, Jesus collected a following of disciples (pupils) which he taught, then later appointed as his Twelve Apostles.

Matthew 10:2,

Now the twelve apostles are these; The first is Simon, who Jesus called by the surname Peter, and Andrew his brother; James the son of Zebedee, and John his brother;

10:3 Philip and Bartholomew; [later referred to as doubting] Thomas, and Matthew the publican; James the son of Alphaeus, and Lebbaeus, whose surname was Thaddaeus [by which he was most often referred];

*10:4 Simon, called Zelote, the Canaan-
ite; and Judas Iscariot, the tax collec-
tor and traitor who betrayed Jesus by
a kiss.*

These twelve apostles, often referred to as disciples, were Christ's messengers, whom he sent forth to preach about the kingdom of heaven. To gain the trust and recognition of followers, Jesus gave the apostles power to work miracles; heal all sickness, cleanse the lepers, cast out evil spirits (exorcise demons) and raise the dead.

John 20:21,

*Then Jesus said to them again, Peace
be to you! Just as the Father has sent
me forth, I am sending you.*

*20:22 And when he had said this, He
breathed on them and said to them, Receive the Holy Spirit!*

*20:23 If you forgive anyone their sins,
they are forgiven; if you do not forgive
them, they are retained.*

Matthew 10:1

*And Jesus called his twelve disciples to
him and gave them the power and authority to drive out unclean evil spirits
to cure every kind of disease, sickness
and infirmity.*

Luke 9:1, (KJV)

*Then he called his twelve disciples to-
gether, and gave them power and authority over all devils, and to cure dis-
eases.*

9:2 And he sent them to preach the kingdom of God, and to heal the sick.

Jesus used his authority to do God's will and taught his disciples [apostles] how to command their will by the authority given them by Him.

Matthew 9:35 (KJV)

And Jesus went about all the cities and villages, teaching in their synagogues and proclaiming the gospel of the kingdom, and healing every sickness and every disease among the people.

Matthew 7:28

And so it was, when Jesus had finished these sayings [the Sermon on the Mount] that the crowds of people were astonished and overwhelmed with wonder at His teaching,

It has been noted that Jesus spoke with charismatic authority. He spoke simply but gave examples by His stories to provoke deep thought. Jesus often spoke in parables and aphorisms, championed the poor and oppressed, but mainly taught about the Kingdom of God.

Matthew 13:10,

The disciples came to Him and said, Why do You speak to them in parables?

13:11 And He replied, To you the knowledge of the secrets and mysteries of the kingdom of heaven has been given but to them it has not been given.

13:12 For whoever has spiritual knowledge, to him will more be given so that he will have abundance; but whoever has not, even what he has will be taken away.

13:13 The reason I speak in parables is because having the power of seeing, they see not; and having the power of hearing they hear not, and neither shall they understand.

13:14 Thereby fulfilled is the prophecy of Isaiah which says: You will hear but never grasp or understand; and you will look but never see or perceive.

13:15 For this nation's heart has become hardened, and their ears have difficulty hearing, and their eyes they have tightly closed, so that they cannot see with their eyes, and cannot hear with their ears, nor understand with their heart, and turn to me and let me heal them.

13:16 But blessed are you, happy, fortunate, and to be envied; and your eyes because they do see, and your ears because they do hear.

13:17 I tell you truthfully, many prophets and righteous men have desired to see what you see, and did not see it; and to hear what you hear, and did not hear it.

Healings and Miracles

Luke 10:19

Behold! I have given you authority and power to trample upon serpents and scorpions, and [physical and mental strength and ability to overcome] all the power that the enemy possesses; that nothing shall in any way harm you.

Once again, Jesus explained we have authority to command things in His name. For example, say, "by the authority given me in Christ, I command..." Jesus did not pray for the sick but commanded out loud the sickness "leave," "be healed" or "be gone." Often such commands were accompanied by touching the afflicted parts of the body or instead, the top of one's head.

Jesus performed healings and miracles because His reputation preceded Him and His services were in great demand. Miracles were performed for the rich and the poor for there was no price attached: They could not and cannot be purchased. Miracles take faith, not finances to be materialized. Yes, miracles occur no less frequently today than in centuries past. And they come in all sizes.

Modern day miracles is a book in itself: And there are several good ones on the market. For your benefit I have listed here a few of the healing miracles Jesus performed. But be aware that sometimes a broken body, for example, cannot receive a miracle. It is our faith that heals us but sometimes not until the heart is healed first.

Luke 4:40 (NIV)

When the sun was setting, the people brought to Jesus all who had various kinds of sickness, and laying his hands on each one, he healed them.

Luke 18:42 (ASV)

And Jesus said unto him, Receive thy sight; thy faith hath made thee whole.

Matthew 17:18

And Jesus rebuked the demon, and it came out of him, and the boy was cured from that moment.

Luke 9:42

And even while the boy was coming, the demon threw him down and [completely] convulsed him. But Jesus censured and severely rebuked the unclean spirit and healed the child and gave him back to his father.

Matthew 9:20, (ASV)

And behold, a woman, who had an issue of blood twelve years, came behind him, and touched the border of his garment:

9:21 for she said within herself, If I do but touch his garment, I shall be made whole.

9:22 But Jesus turning and seeing her said, Daughter, be of good cheer; thy faith hath made thee whole. And the woman was made whole from that hour.

Matthew 8:5,

As Jesus went into Capernaum a city on the western shore of the Sea of Galilee a Roman officer (centurion) came up to Him pleading

8:6 And saying, Lord, my servant boy is lying at the house paralyzed and distressed with terrible pains.

8:7 And Jesus said to him, I will come and heal him.

8:8 But the officer said, Lord, I am not worthy to have you come under my roof. Just speak the word and my servant boy will be healed.

8:13 Then to the Roman officer Jesus said, Go; it shall be done for you because you have believed. And the servant boy was healed at that very moment.

Jesus' ministry was His teachings and His sermons, and with His charisma, He attracted the multitudes. However, His ability to perform miracles made Him in demand almost wherever He went. Although the majority of His miracles were physical healings including curing the blind and the lepers, He also raised the dead and exorcised demons. Jesus' miracles and teachings often involve food; either feasting or fasting.

Luke 11:14

Now Jesus was driving out a demon that was dumb [speechless]; and it happened that when the demon had gone out, the mute man spoke. And the crowds marveled.

Miracles for the twenty-first century might include removing all urges to continue any bad habit such as smoking, drinking, drugs, or overeating. Or coming to the rescue by fixing a computer, TV, car or cell phone. Or to find Freddie, a frightened older house cat who survived a second-story fall and then became lost in the wet and wild woods for a month.

Every area of our lives are under His watchful eye. Just ask; and believe. Miracles still happen in today's world. Finance is a big area and the one in which God tells us to test him. Learn the laws and rules of money spelled out in the bible and follow them. Then test him. He tells us to do our part (what we are able to do) and He will do what we are unable to do. For me, that meant when I received medical bills totaling many thousands of dollars recently, I started making monthly payment arrangements on the small individual bills, and soon thereafter received a letter from the hospital saying they had "forgiven" the biggest bill of about $12,000.

I have been forgiven much and I am thankful.

Salvation

Deuteronomy 30:19 (KJV)
I call heaven and earth to record this day against you, that I have set before you life and death, blessing and cursing: therefore choose life, that both thou and thy seed [children and future generations] may live:

From time to time throughout my early adulthood I considered attending church and reestablishing the relationship I had with God when I was a child. Frankly, I could never find a congregation compatible with my way of thinking; let alone any who were compatible amongst themselves. Factions of every denomination, it seemed, voiced their beliefs spiritually, socially and politically. It didn't take me long to realize that I didn't fit in with any of these congregations (and I still don't) because I won't be told what and how to believe.

Back in the "good old" days there were no responses such as applause or interactions of any kind from the congregation. Churches mimicked tombs; cold and silent. Preachers yelled their sermons at us (too many still do), probably to keep us awake. They called us sinners, talked about washing in the blood, hell fire and brimstone, Christ's crucifixion, speaking in tongues, fearing God, tithing and similar topics which offered little or no practical, life-enhancing or uplifting benefit.

Frankly, I was grossly offended when referred to as a sinner because I never considered myself as such. After all, I was a good person who tried to live right and pretty much do the right thing. How dare those righteous men condemn me!

It was about the time I attained "grandma hood" some decades later that I understood about sin. We are considered sinners in God's eyes not only because of what we might do but because of who we are. Simply, we are human beings who are not perfect. God is perfect but there are flaws (sins) in our makeup which we inherited from Eve's Adam. We are not only sinners because we sin but also, we sin because we are sinners.

The gist of it all is that we come short of the glory of God (Christ) and cannot come into His presence without being cleansed first.

> ***Romans 10:9 (NIV)***
>
> *If you confess with your mouth, "Jesus is Lord" and believe in your heart that God raised him from the dead, you will be saved.*

God made us purposefully with the capability of free choice. When we sin by thought or deed we are a breaker of God's laws. We cannot make up for our sins (flaws) and we cannot save ourselves. The bible teaches us Jesus died to set us free of our sins and gave us eternal life. Which means the price has been paid for and the gift has been given to each of us. Our next step is to receive by confessing our sins and asking (believing) for forgiveness.

> ***II Corinthians 5:21 (ASV)***
>
> *Him who knew no sin he made to be sin on our behalf; that we might become the righteousness of God in him.*

Hebrews 2:14,

Because God's children are made of flesh and blood [human beings] the Son also became a flesh and blood human being. For only then could he die, and thereby by dying could he break the power of death held the by devil.

2:15 This was the only way could he set free all who have lived their lives in bondage to the fear of dying.

More good news is that God has given us His grace which is unmerited favor, and His mercy. Although we didn't earn it He has chosen not to remember our sins as if erasing them from memory. Additionally, any of our sins recorded in the Book of Life have been erased forever which is why we will be in attendance but not on trial on judgment day.

*Titus 3:5,

not by works done in righteousness, which we did ourselves, but according to his mercy he saved us, through [the washing away of our sins which gives us new birth and] new life through the Holy Spirit,

3:6 which he [generously] poured out upon us richly, through Jesus Christ our Saviour;

It's true we *repent* when we confess our sins and ask (believe for) forgiveness. While this is true because we are regretful for past conduct or thoughts, the basis of repentance includes a *change* of mind; a new direction or a new way of life and a commitment to Christ. God will then change our way of thinking; transforming us into a newly spirited soul. We will only then learn the perfect and wondrous plans God has for us.

> ***II Corinthians 5:17*** *again,*
>
> *Therefore, if anyone is in Christ, he is a new creature [creation]; the old things have passed away; behold, all things have become new.*
>
> ***Colossians 2:6***
>
> *Now just as you received Christ Jesus as your Lord, you must continue to live in him,*
>
> ***2:7** be rooted in him, let your lives be built up and strengthened in your faith which will grow strong, and you will overflow with thankfulness.*
>
> ***2:8** Beware that no one captivates you with empty and deceptive philosophies of human and/or worldly capabilities or principals rather than on Christ.*

Understanding God's Sacrifice

God is conforming us to the likes of Jesus. By so doing, we are now able to be in His Holy presence.

> ***Romans 3:22,***
>
> *No matter who we are, we are now righteous in God's sight through our belief and faith in Jesus Christ.*
>
> *3:23 For we have all sinned and fallen short of God's glorious perfection.*
>
> *3:24 Yet, by His grace, God declared we are righteous, through Christ Jesus, who redeemed us from our sins.*
>
> *3:25 God presented His son Jesus as the sacrifice for sin of mankind. This was God's way of making believers righteous and also being fair to those who sinned in times past but were passed over and not punished.*
>
> *3:26 God did this to demonstrate His righteousness; that he is fair and just; and that sinners who have faith in Jesus are right in His sight.*

Above all else, we know that God is a loving, fair and just God. He will never do anything *to* us; only *for* us. So, why then, would God not allow some people into heaven just because they were adversely born into obscurity. What about people who live in remote, non-civilized corners of the world (or even in our hometowns) who have never heard of Jesus? Faithful church-going Christians have reassured me repeatedly that these innocent souls are the reason churches and others support field missionaries.

Sorry. Not a good-enough answer for me. That doesn't sound loving, fair or just. I needed a better answer before I would be willing to get involved. So, I made a deal with God to clue me in or write me off.

Here I am again rocking the proverbial boat. But, at the risk of capsizing legalistic Christian concepts, the following is what He presented in His eloquence to me.

"Through means because of"

Much, too simple.Too easy an answer for such a big question. Wow! What does it really mean?

The example given me was: Come to Him *through* Jesus Christ means *because of* Jesus Christ. In other words, it is *because of* Jesus' existence (including his life, death and resurrection) and his love for us that we are saved.

> ***Acts 15:11***
>
> *We believe that through the undeserved grace of the Lord Jesus Christ we shall all be saved in the same way.*
>
> ***John 14:6 (NIV)***
>
> *Jesus answered, "I am the way and the truth and the life. No one comes to the Father except through me.*

Yes, *because of* Jesus even souls belonging to small distant tribes who have never even heard His name can be saved. And, *because of* Jesus even souls who lived and died a few thousand years before Him may choose eternal life. Now, anyone who *believes in* God, has the opportunity to choose everlasting life.

Civilizations everywhere throughout the world's history have revered a God. Many civilizations have had many gods, at least until they have become intelligent enough or educated enough to understand that a blade of grass, a golden idol or a sacred ram doesn't have the wherewithal to be Godlike. Just because a prophet, mystic or religious leader once established a religion is no reason to believe they were sent from God. If, however, that same God called the prophet His son; gave Him His powers including healing abilities; raised Him from the dead and resurrected Him into heaven, then it would be worth considering the significance.

Most historians accept that Pontius Pilate (the Roman Prefect of Judaea between 26 and 36 AD) ordered Christ at the age of about thirty three crucified in Jerusalem. He was charged with sedition (dictionary described as "conduct or language inciting discontent or rebellion against a government") which in reality meant treason against the Roman Empire.

The presence and persecution of Christians in first-century Rome is well documented. The violent resistance to Roman rule in distant lands is also well documented. Gospels tell us Jesus was executed on political charges because this charismatic leader was feared a potential troublemaker.

It was on a Sabbath holy day that Jesus acted to raise Lazarus from the dead. Besides inciting Jewish leaders, it gave them cause to finally plan his death. Both the Jewish and Roman authorities seemed threatened by Him.This Jewish peasant named Jesus, it was rumored, was assuming titles such as "Son of God," "God," "The Prince of Peace," "Saviour," and "Redeemer"which were reserved for the identity of the Roman emperor.

The bible teaches us Jesus died to set us free of our sins and give us eternal life.

II Corinthians 5:15 (ASV)

and he died for all, that they that live should no longer live unto themselves, but unto him who for their sakes died and rose again.

One of the earliest texts from the mid-first century which is still in existence (not destroyed or lost) is one with Paul's letters which confirms Jesus' crucifixion. The gospel of St. John finishes His life's work here on earth with:

John 19:30 (ASV)

When Jesus therefore had received the vinegar, he said, It is finished: and he bowed his head, and gave up his spirit.

Resurrection and Ascension

Romans 1:4

And declared to be the Son of God with power, when he was raised from the dead by the Spirit of Holiness: Jesus Christ our Lord.

Because of the Resurrection from the dead by the Holy Spirit, Jesus is declared to be the Son of God with almighty powers. What make Jesus so very different from any other spiritual or religious leader is that no other has ever risen from the dead. No other has proven their immortality. They have all shown themselves to be mortally human and thereby not godlike or almighty powerful.

Revelation 1:17, (KJV)

And when I saw him, I fell at his feet as dead. And he laid his right hand upon me, saying unto me, Fear not; I am the first and the last:

1:18 I am he that liveth, and was dead, and, behold, I am alive for evermore, Amen; and have the keys of hell and of death.

For forty days the risen Jesus was acknowledged by more than five hundred observers who attested to his existence. In the gospel of St. Mark, Jesus appears to Mary Magdalene, to two disciples in the country, and to the eleven apostles. It is then that Jesus commissions them to go forward to announce the gospel, baptize, and work miracles.

In the gospel of St. Matthew, Jesus appears to Mary Magdalene and the eleven apostles on a mountain, at which point he commissions them to enlist followers, baptize, and teach to the whole world what He taught (the Great Commission).

> **Mark 16:14**
> *Jesus appeared to the eleven as they sat reclining at the table; and He rebuked their unbelief and hardness of heart because they had not believed those who had seen Him after He had resurrected.*
>
> ***Acts 10:41,**
> *...We were those chosen to eat and drink with him after he rose from the dead.*
>
> *10:42 And he commanded us to preach to people everywhere and to testify that Jesus is the one appointed by God to be the judge of the living and the dead.*
>
> *10:43 He is the one the prophets testified about: Saying that whosoever shall believe in him will have their sins forgiven.*

In John, Jesus appears to Mary Magdalene and to the eleven. There He demonstrates his physical reality to doubting Thomas. The books of Mark and Luke both tell us Jesus ascends to the heavens:

On the 40th day after the Resurrection of Jesus, Christ ascended into heaven by bodily rising upward.

> *Acts 2:32 (KJV)*
> *This Jesus hath God raised up, whereof we all are witnesses.*
> *Philippians 3:20*
> *But we are citizens of heaven, where the Lord Jesus Christ lives, And from where we are eagerly waiting for him to return as our Savior.*
> *II Corinthians 4:14*
> *We know that God who raised up the Lord Jesus, will raise us up also with Jesus. He will bring us all together to present ourselves before God.*

Jesus preached that He will return leading an apocalyptic crusade at the end times of our current world age. Signs preceding His return will include natural disasters such as earthquakes and weather changes which will produce floods, droughts, and famines. There will be world-wide financial and social tribulations and religious persecutions. Evil will overcome and deceive good; including false Messiahs. Jesus warns His faithful believers to look for signs from above of His return.

> *Revelation 22:7*
> *Behold, When I [Jesus speaking] come quickly: Blessed are they who obey the words of the prophecy written in this book [the Bible].*
> *Revelation 22:21 (KJV)*
> *The grace of our Lord Jesus Christ be-with you all. Amen.*

His Purpose

In the Gospel of John, Chapter 10 and Verse 10, Jesus said of his divine purpose, "I came that they may have life, and have it abundantly." But John states that Jesus came so that "those who believed in him would have eternal life." Could it be that these two statements have the same meaning? I think it's usual to initially think of abundance in tangible terms limited by earthly quantities such as time and space. If, however, we remove the earthly limitations, we are gifted with an unqualified life without an ending.

Contending for one of, if not *the* most read and most well-known scriptures of the New Testament (and one I memorized as a child at the knee of my late and dear, great aunt Kate) is the following verse where we are told Jesus died to set us free and give us everlasting life.

> **John 3:16 (ASV)*
>
> *For God so loved the world, that he gave his only begotten Son, that whosoever believeth on him should not perish, but have eternal life.*
>
> **Proverbs 22:6 (KJV)**
>
> *Train up a child in the way he should go and when he is old, he will not depart from it.*

While Luke proclaimed that Jesus was sent to "preach the good news of the Kingdom of God," Mark declares that Jesus' purpose was to "give his life as a ransom for many."And then, almost at the very end of the New Testament we find the following proclamation.

*I John 5:20

We know that the Son of God has come, and he has given us understanding so that we may know him who is the true God. Now we live in relationship with the true God because we live in relationship with his Son, Jesus Christ. He is the only true God: He is eternal life.

*John 6:29

Jesus replied, This is the work [service] that God asks of you: that you believe in the One Whom He has sent [that you cleave to, trust, rely on, and have faith in Him].

Chapter 3

Knowing The Holy Spirit

John 4:24 (KJV)
God is a Spirit: and they that worship him must worship him in spirit and in truth.

The Holy Spirit is sometimes referred to by other names such as the Holy Ghost, the Helper, the Spirit of truth, the comforter, the counselor, the Intercessor, the Advocate, strengthener or standby. By whatever title we use, we have the presence of God with us when we have the Holy Spirit with us.

The Holy Spirit is separate and distinct but equal with God the Father and Jesus the Son. The Holy Spirit is not just the spirit of God, but a being who has a will. He shows mercy and compassion. He will walk with us through every situation. Our gut level reactions are led by the Holy Spirit.

I Corinthians 2:10 (NLT)
But it was to us that God revealed these things by his Spirit. For his Spirit searches out everything and shows us God's deep secrets.

The Holy spirit works beyond intellect and beyond reason. He works with our conscious and our subconscious minds. He speaks to us, He tells us, shows us or warns us of things that are to come. He acts on our behalf, He comforts us, He intercedes if needed, and He commands.

70

The seventeenth century French philosopher Blasé Pascal expressed the "something missing" emptiness in our lives and in our hearts that many of us recognize as the "God-sized hole" in each of us.

When we believe and acknowledge that God is our heavenly Father whose son Jesus was crucified for the sins of mankind, we must ask God's forgiveness. He will then send the Holy Spirit to dwell within us and to guide us in our daily lives.

It is the Holy Spirit who will renew our character, thoughts, and emotions when we have received our new life in Christ. We might think of it as cleansing ourselves to make us righteous which is necessary because God can only dwell within holy ground. If we become righteous because of the Holy Spirit, we are productive and fruitful all the days of our lives. We enjoy Spirit-driven success.

> *Acts 2:38 (ASV)*
>
> *And Peter said unto them, Repent ye, and be baptized every one of you in the name of Jesus Christ unto the remission.[forgiveness] of your sins; and ye shall receive the gift of the Holy Spirit.*
>
> *John 16:7 (ASV)*
>
> *[Jesus talking to his disciples]*
> *Nevertheless I tell you the truth: It is expedient for you that I go away; for if I go not away, the Comforter [Holy Spirit] will not come unto you; but if I go, I will send him unto you.*

After the influence of the Holy Spirit comes upon us, we feel powerful. Through the Holy Spirit God gives us supernatural abilities to be successful in our earthly life. Ever wonder why some tasks are exceptionally easy for some people when the same tasks are often difficult for most of us. Or why everything seems to go wrong all the time while some people seem to be so lucky all the time. We've all seen those who seem to breeze through their life's problems when some of us suffer or struggle so desperately in ours.

> ### Acts 1:8 (ASV)
> *But ye shall receive power, when the Holy Spirit is come upon you: and ye shall be my [God's] witnesses both in Jerusalem, and in all Judaea and Samaria, and unto the uttermost part [ends] of the earth.*

Why do some people have such easy lives? Why are they so blessed? The Holy Spirit is often called the Helper just for these reasons. But, he is so much more. Actually, He guides everything about our life. He is responsible for our thinking and speaking differently about all areas of our life without making a conscious effort. He forms and delivers the sentences we speak in difficult situations. He also helps us offer perfect prayers.

Fruits of the Holy Spirit

The Holy Spirit also gives us gifts referred to in the Bible as fruits. The fruits of true love, joy and peace can be available to all on earth and no one can take them away from us. These will remain with our soul after death.

If we reject these gifts by expressing life through hatred, misery and hostilities, then these negative characteristics will remain with our soul (I venture to guess someplace other than heaven) after death. When we accept the remaining six gifts of patience, kindness, goodness, faithfulness, gentleness and self-control we become more Christ-like; a more perfect being who has a positive impact on our world. Bearing good fruit every day will make a positive difference in people's lives.

> *Galatians 5:22, (KJV)*
> *But the fruit of the Spirit [fruit that the holy spirit produces in our lives] is love, joy,peace, longsuffering [patience], gentleness, goodness, faith,*
> *5:23 Meekness [kindness], temperance [self-control]: against such there is no law.*

Personally, the Holy Spirit was represented to me in the form of a dove in a dream. For several years my dreams were haunted by my deceased ex-husband who persistently requested I forgive him for his devastating and scandalous behaviors during his lifetime. Frankly, I was annoyed by his intrusions into my dreams and my new life. Eventually, I selfishly agreed to his request just to put an end to his nightmarish visitations.

In this dream, my ex-husband left my presence for four or five seconds, and then returned with a large round object in one hand which I thought looked like a geode. You know, one of those rocks you break open with a hammer and find beautiful crystals growing inside. As the geode rested in his palm, it slowly split apart and began opening, and then, at the same time the geode vanished, a dove appeared from within.

Still wondering what this scoundrel (my ex-husband) was doing in God's heaven, I complained loudly about how unimpressed I was with an everyday pigeon-colored gray dove instead of him bringing me a beautiful white dove. At once he turned to leave a second time for another four or five seconds which I calculated in dream time. You guessed it. He returned with another crystallized geode, this time abiding a beautiful pure white dove.

The dove was mine only briefly, before both the dove and the dream vanished into deep sleep. When I awoke in the morning, however, I knew that somehow, everything in my life would be forever changed.

Occasionally, a dream seems so real to life, that I have trouble believing if it really did happen. In this instance every small detail was so vivid I felt compelled to research matters further. The following weeks were spent looking up every Bible verse mentioning doves which is how I eventually learned about the Holy Spirit who is not only shy and sensitive like a dove but represented by the dove.

Matthew 3:16 (KJV)

And Jesus, when he was baptized, went up straightway out of the water: and, lo, the heavens were opened unto him, and he saw the Spirit of God descending like a dove, and lighting upon him:

Initially I was appalled this scoundrel, my ex-husband, would be allowed into heaven and frankly, a little miffed at God for letting him in. After years of his relentless begging my forgiveness in my dreams, it wasn't until after I agreed to forgive him that I finally got some restful sleep. Although he still disturbed my dreams, thankfully it was less often and less nightmarish. Then the proverbial ton of bricks hit me as I realized my ex-husband never cared whether or not I forgave him.

God showed me that my forgiveness was not for the benefit of my ex-husband but for my own. Unknown to me then, I was unable to receive the Holy Spirit until I had given my forgiveness (and thereby prepared or cleansed myself). It was important that I held no grudges or discontent. How good God is. He knew I now would no longer have any reason to significantly care about worlds past.

From that one experience I had several major lessons to learn. Most importantly, God had proved to me again that He truly does exist (live) and that growth begins with spiritual sight. I will never, ever again doubt Him.

Secondly, I am convinced that God may sometimes communicate with us through our dreams.

Thirdly, the Holy Spirit cannot operate successfully within us if we hold onto unforgiveness. We must not only ask for forgiveness but we must give forgiveness to others as well. This is a "big one" that took me a few weeks to figure out and even longer to make a part of my daily life. With some of the people in my life it is a continuing struggle.

To those of us who ask forgiveness, God forgives our transgressions and they are erased from his memory forever. Upon asking for forgiveness we may become born anew and become a child of God. Forgiveness is so vitally important. But we must also forgive others or God may not forgive us. Certainly if we don't forgive others we will not become a son of God and be spirit filled. There are many children of God but few sons.

Matthew 22:14 (KJV)

For many are called but few are chosen.

Now, my deceased ex-husband was a major *Ten Commandment* breaker (among other despicable behaviors) who believed in God's existence but only trusted and believed *in* himself. Yes, he was the everyday garden variety of sociopath without conscience who was ruthless in his efforts to control and manipulate everyone and everything.

Although I now know that our spirit and soul are returned to God when our bodies die, I was secretly relieved to learn that my ex-husband had not yet "made" it to heaven. He's in a type of holding pattern waiting to appear before God on judgment day. After all, he does have much to explain.

Gifts of the Holy Spirit

God has a purpose for everything. And He has gifts for us which are indescribable.

> *John 15:26, (NLT) [Jesus speaking]*
> *But I will send you the Advocate--the Spirit of truth. He will come to you from the Father and will testify all about me.*
> *15:27 And you must also testify about me because you have been with me from the beginning of my ministry.*

When the Holy Spirit is manifested to believers, he bestows and controls spiritual gifts for everyone. These spiritual gifts are divided among us. Some may receive only one or two and others may receive many gifts, depending on our personal interests and capabilities, our motivations and also on how well we use these gifts. Gifts may be changed or exchanged from time to time. It is the Holy Spirit who decides which gifts each person should have and distributes them. These gifts are given for the common good, for the body of Christ (i.e. the church) but also they are given so we can help one another, as well as for our own good and profit.

> *I Corinthians 12:7 (KJV)*
> *But the manifestation of the Spirit is given to every man to profit withal.*

These spiritual gifts are wisdom, faith, knowledge, healing, prophecy, working of miracles and miraculous powers,discerning of spirits, speaking in tongues and also the interpretation of tongues (languages).

I Corinthians 12:8,

*For to one is given through the Spirit
the word [message] of wisdom [abil-
ity to give wise advice]; and to another
[the power to express] the word of special knowledge and understanding, according to the same Spirit:*

12:9 *to another [is given wonder-
working] faith, in [by] the same [Holy]
Spirit; and to another the extraordi-
nary powers and the gifts of healings,
in [by] the one Spirit;*

12:10 *and to another He gives miraculous powers and the workings of [the
power to perform] miracles; and to another prophecy [and prophetic insight
which is the gift of interpreting His divine will and purpose]; and to another
discerning of [and distinguishing between the utterances and messages and
whether they are of God or false] spirits; to another [speaking in various]
diverse kinds of [unknown] tongues
[languages];and to another the [abil-
ity of] interpretation of tongues [what
is being said]*

The Holy Spirit of God gives these gifts, abilities
and achievements, to each believer individually exactly
as He wills. Each of us has been given at least one very
special gift. The Holy Spirit will guide us into a place
of service using the particular gift(s) He has chosen for
us. He will also give us power and mercy. As His children,

God has promised us that these gifts will follow us all the days of our lives. When we are given a gift (as with a fruit of the spirit), we have to reach out and accept it so we can open it and enjoy it. We have to receive it! Until we do, we can't experience the true blessing of the gift.

It is important to realize that God is not a passive giver. He doesn't give us His gifts and mercy because He feels obligated, and He doesn't give them and then take them back again. We learn how to receive with expectation what God has for us every day. Gifts like these lift us up. They encourage us and fill us with strength. The power of God is in the Holy Spirit and therefore, God's power is ours when we know the Holy Spirit.

Spiritual gifts are not merely given to us for our own benefit or enjoyment but are given to enable us to minister to others. The Holy Spirit will provide us opportunities and will show us how we are to be of service.

Occasionally the Holy Spirit may manifest a particular gift through us to meet a specific need at a particular time. It may be a gift that has never operated in our life before, but when the Spirit puts us in a situation, He will illuminate our mind to meet the need. And, he will never give us more than we are capable of managing.

The Holy Spirit will guide us by truth. He will reveal Jesus Christ and how we can have fellowship with him. With spiritual gifts and power He will inspire and influence our love. It is because we love Christ that God gives us the Holy Spirit and works miracles among us.

Unfortunately, many people miss out on the true wonders of this life because they cannot see beyond themselves or comprehend what they cannot see. Others have closeted themselves from truth. It is very difficult for many who live in a natural world to acknowledge the *super*natural world also exists.

After all, it is so foolishly easy to deny or at least ignore an infinite existence when we are so involved with the immediate world in which we are living...even if it is only our temporary world.

I Corinthians 2:14

But the natural [nonspiritual] man receives not [does not accept or welcome or admit into his heart] the things [the gifts and teachings and revelations] of the Spirit of God: for they are foolishness unto him: neither can he know them [understand or become familiar with them], because they are spiritually discerned [and appreciated.]

Proverbs 27:22

Even if we grind him with mortar and pestle like a shaft of grain, we cannot separate a fool from his foolishness.

If you have an ear, listen to what the Spirit is saying to you. He is the spiritual messenger. He works in our world and in our lives. The Holy Bible is written by the Holy Spirit. Let the Holy Spirit empower you!

Who is Spirit-Filled

John 1:32 (NIV)
Then John gave this testimony: "I saw the Spirit come down from heaven as a dove and remain on him.

When we become Christians or are "born-again" we may or may not immediately become spirit-filled. God may send the gift of the Holy Spirit to dwell within us. The Holy Spirit then is with us always. Some people believe the Holy Spirit fuses with or replaces *our* spirit while others describe Him as standing at our side, living within our hearts, living within our heads or smack in the center of our being.

Galatians 4:6 (ASV)
And because ye are sons [not merely children but sons of God], God sent forth the Spirit of his Son into our hearts, crying Abba, Father.

The Holy Spirit steps into our spirit (and body and soul) and directs it forever. God thereby gives us a new spirit and a new heart which He lives in as his own. The Holy Spirit saturates us with His presence, He anoints us and empowers us. Not only is He always with us but He is always at ready, waiting for us to require His guidance. He frequently forms the words we speak without our knowing ahead of time what we are going to say. This He does especially in life's difficult situations.

The Holy Spirit takes up residence within "believers" because He knows the purpose (mind of God) for our lives. Even if our conscious mind has not been spiritually active, the Holy Spirit works in conjunction with our conscious mind which includes capabilities beyond our intellect and beyond our reason. Often the Holy Spirit also manifests those gut-level reactions when he leads us.

Our entire lives become elevated. He powerfully guides us in prayer. And sometimes that prayer continues without ceasing through sleep and dreams. We become baptized with the Holy Spirit until our earthly bodies die. And when our bodies die, our spirit is immediately reunited with God.

> *Ecclesiastes 12:7 (ASV) again,*
> *and the dust returneth to the earth [out of which God made man's body] as it was, and the spirit returneth unto God who gave it.*

If we are not immediately spirit-filled, and we have truly made a commitment to God, we may have to deal with an issue such as forgiveness first. No one is able to receive the spirit until they conform their hearts. And of course, speaking against the Holy Spirit will never be accepted. It's a deal-breaker!

> *Matthew 12:32 (ASV)*
> *And whosoever shall speak a word against the Son of man, it shall be for-given him: but whosoever shall speak against the Holy Spirit, it shall not be forgiven him, neither in this world, nor in the world to come.*

The New Testament tells us that every person who is born again, who receives Jesus into their heart has the Holy Spirit in a measure. But it also tells us we need more than a measure: we need a fullness of the power of the Holy Spirit. We get filled with the Holy Spirit by faith.

We receive power when the Holy Spirit comes upon us and we develop a desire to become a witness throughout the world. We watch for such opportunities.

But just being born again isn't enough. If we are born again but not spirit filled, we are living a lower life than the life God has made available to us. If we are not putting God first we cannot truly enjoy living. Then again, if we are doing something to grieve the spirit we cannot become spirit filled until we forgive and are forgiven. For example, types of self-destructive behaviors which will cause the dove to flutter away because God is grieved are as follows:

If we treat people badly

If we talk badly about people

If we gossip

If our talk makes someone look bad

If we want to hurt or punish someone

If we harbor bitterness or vengeance

If we have not forgiven those who hurt us

The Holy Spirit is sent by the Father and/or Son. He comforts us in times of trial, provides the right words for us to say, He helps us in our weaknesses and guides us through the passage of death. God grants boldness to believers who are spirit-filled.

The Holy Spirit guides us in our prayers and gives us an unlimited prayer life.

Romans 8:26,

The Holy Spirit assists us when we don't know how to pray and for what to pray. The Holy Spirit prays and pleads with God in our behalf; not with words

but with yearnings and groanings too deep to be expressed in words.
8:27 *Father God who knows the hearts of all men understands when the Holy Spirit intercedes and pleads for believers in harmony with God's own will.*

If you are looking for a church to visit or join, my personal preference is a bible-based church. Spirit-filled churches, just like spirit-filled believers, read (live in) the word, pray, receive miracles, have unity, are givers, trust God for provision and nurture each other.

Life's Purpose

Jeremiah 33:3 (KJV)
Call unto me, and I will answer thee, and show thee great and mighty things, which thou knowest not.

Before we were born, our divine destiny was determined by God. Our purpose or destiny is something we like to do, something we are good at doing. Our purpose will create a passion burning inside of us; a sanctioned and continuing need to be productive. Often it begins as a dream. If we discover our gift it will lead us to our purpose, to our destiny. The gifts of the spirit are the gifts that will be a part of our calling, our purpose.

I Peter 4:11
If you have the God-given gift of speaking then speak as though God himself were speaking through you. If you have the gift of ministering to and helping others, then do it with all the strength, energy and ability that God gives [supplies] to you. Thus, everything you do will bring glory to God through Jesus Christ. All glory and power to him forever and ever! Amen.

We are here on this earth for a reason. A wonderful reason other than to just take up space or consume the environment. Life is not about us getting our way; rather, what is best for all. Life is bigger than the individuals who make it up. God has something for each of us to do in our life. We can only be truly fulfilled by learning and following God's purpose.

God tells us "I have a plan for your life." He says there is a purpose we are here on this earth and if we let Him direct us, He will show us the purpose for our life. He also promises to give us fulfillment and joy unspeakable. He will enable us to do all that we need to do. How glorious it is that He promises all things which we hope for *will* come to pass in our life! What do we have to do to receive it? We have to give our life to Jesus; let Him become our Lord. From that moment on, He will take us on an adventure beyond anything we can imagine

Romans 8:28 (KJV)

And we know that all things work together for good to them that love God, to them who are the called according to his purpose.

God will place new desires and aspirations in our hearts. When He makes us spiritually whole, He gives us new priorities, new values, new desires. He gives us holy desires, desires for spiritual blessings, a hunger for his word and desires that only He can fulfill. And He delights in fulfilling them.

Jeremiah 29:11 (KJV)

For I know the thoughts that I think toward you [plans I have for you], saith the LORD, thoughts of peace [plans to prosper you] and not of evil [not to harm you], to give you an expected end [plans to give you hope and a future].

Significantly, He gives our life meaning and purpose and He guides us to fulfill that purpose. The Holy Spirit who is filled with love and goodness will lead us to and through our purpose in life.

Psalm 138:8

The Lord will fulfill his plans and purpose for my life which concern me; for your merciful and faithful love, O LORD, endures forever..

Book III

Eternally Yours

Book III

Eternally Yours

Enjoy your life's journey on the way to your destination.

In I Thessalonians, Chapter 4, we learn that true believers do not experience the "sting of death" that non-Christians feel when mourning the loss of a loved one through death. Non-Christians grieve because they realize their mortality and thereby have no hope to cling to. Christians however, refer to the loss as temporary, as a "passing" or "passing away" because they know that they are passing into a glorious eternal life which they anxiously look forward to experiencing.

There is much talk these days in Christian circles (as there has also been in centuries past) of this earth's age coming to an end. The world as we know it will one day be no more. In these *last days* however, almost if not all of the criteria outlined in the Bible, especially in the books of Daniel and Revelation, have been met.

Technically, I was born a few years before this last generation of the *last days*: Born just shortly before the nation of Israel was re-established in 1948. With God's Grace I may not die here on earth but instead, experience the *Rapture*. Meaning, to be able to stay alive long enough to become transfigured and caught up in the clouds to meet Jesus.

Those of previous generations whose souls and spirits are in heaven (those who have died following and believing in Jesus), will return with the coming of the Lord. Those of us who are alive at His coming shall join Jesus and the generations past.

I Corinthians 15:52 (NLT)

It will happen in a moment, in the blink of an eye, when the last trumpet is blown. For when the trumpet sounds, those who have died will be raised [awakened] to live forever. And we who are living will also be transformed [transfigured].

I Thessalonians 4:16-18 (KJV)

For the Lord himself shall descend [come down] from heaven with a shout [loud command], with the voice of the archangel, and with the trumpet [call] of God: and the dead in Christ shall rise [arise from sleep] first.

4:17 Then we who are alive and remain shall be caught up together with them in the clouds, to meet the Lord in the air: and so will we forever be with the Lord.

4:18 Therefore encourage [comfort] one another with these words.

Chapter 1

Heaven

Revelation 3:5 (ASV)
*He that overcometh shall thus be ar-
rayed in white garments; and I will in
no wise blot his name out of the book
of life, and I will confess his name before my Father, and before his angels.*

I've heard it mentioned on television recently that
(70%) seventy percent of people in the United States believe
there is a heaven. And five percent have had near-death (or
afterlife) experiences which is why they believe they have
touched upon the life hereafter. While a few of those people
describe their journey as a hellish tormenting nightmare,
most describe it as a heavenly presence of peace and love,
filled with bright white light.

Those who enter the light describe an all-encompassing
peace in a paradise setting, usually with departed loved
ones present. More importantly, they profess a desire to
remain in this unknown bliss rather than a willingness to
return to their life and loved ones in 'reality.'

Hebrews 12:2 (ASV)
*...and hath sat down at the right hand
of the throne of God. (In the place of
honor beside God)*

Heaven is often described as a peaceful, music-filled
paradise where angelic hosts, saints (God's devoted souls)
gowned in fine white linen from head to toe and a multitude

of believers are worshiping God with one voice in a heavenly language (tongue). Facing towards His presence in a pure white radiance of light and warmth, Saint Stephan describes in Acts how he saw its' glory (splendor and majesty).

> ### Acts 7:55, (ASV)
> *But he, being full of the Holy Spirit, looked up steadfastly into heaven, and saw the glory of God, and Jesus standing on the right hand of God,*
> *7:56 and said, Behold, I see the heavens opened, and the Son of Man standing on the right hand of God.*
> ### Revelation 22:5 (ASV)
> *And there shall be night no more; and they need no light of lamp, neither light of sun; for the Lord God shall give them light: and they shall reign for ever and ever.*

In heaven there is no darkness, no nighttime, no time at all...only the moment. In heaven our souls and spirits never sleep, they don't age or get old, they don't have health problems or pain and they don't die. These days when I look in a mirror, I reflect an aging grandmother but if asked how old I feel, I would have to answer somewhere between twenty eight and thirty two years old. It is just my body, not my soul or spirit, who looks and feels like a sixty-five year old grandma.

> ### Luke 20:34 (ASV)
> *And Jesus said unto them, The sons of this world marry, and are given in marriage:*

20:35 but they that are accounted worthy to attain to that world, and the resurrection from the dead, neither marry, nor are given in marriage:

20:36 for neither can they die any more: for they are equal to the angels and are sons of God.

In paradise there are no marriage or family situations or personal problems: No complaints or complainers; no bills, no debt, no banks or any financial problems; no hate, no crime or other social problems; no national problems and no wars; and no tears. There is no fear. Heaven is a place of joy!

Heaven is a place to worship God. It is a place of love and joy for those with pure hearts. Descriptions of the new heavens and the new earth are throughout the Books of Isaiah and Revelation. It's beauty is beyond our senses; beauty and colors beyond what we can see or visualize and musical sounds beyond what we can hear or imagine. Even St. John was unable to put into adequate words his description of heaven when he likened it to an entire city of transparent golden glass.

When our physical bodies die, our spirit immediately returns to God, as does our soul return into His presence. Our souls will still be our personality developed from an accumulation of our experiences, but in heaven we will be ourselves without any sin. But we will not be souls without bodies. We will put on heavenly bodies which will be without defect. In God's presence, we will be transfigured into His perfect likeness.

Ecclesiastes 12:7 (ASV)

...and the dust returneth to the earth as it was, and the spirit returneth unto God who gave it.

Matthew 17:1, (ASV)

And after six days Jesus taketh with him Peter, and James, and John his brother, and bringeth them up into a high mountain apart:

17:2 and he was transfigured before them; and his face did shine as the sun, and his garments became [brilliant] white as the light.

Children younger than the age of accountability (no matter how old in years) are welcomed into heaven. While some eight year olds know the difference between right and wrong, it may take others years longer to develop. Mercifully, God considers all who are mentally and otherwise challenged. Since we don't age in heaven, it seems reasonable that everyone in perfect heavenly bodies will probably be in the same age group...say perhaps the early thirties or the same age as Jesus when he ascended to heaven.

I remember hearing Billy Graham explain how we are going to heaven by the grace and mercy of God and how he was looking forward to eventually being ushered to the Lord by an angel. Although I had never given that any thought before, I am sure God would be elated to assign an angel escort to Rev. Graham.

I personally expect to see in heaven most of the people I have known here on earth, past and present. Unfortunately, too many people I care for deeply will not attain heavenly bliss either because of their ignorance, pig-headed stubbornness (inherited from my side of the family) and/or lack of faith in anything other than themselves (ego). Fortunately, in heaven we will have no memory of those not with us in the hereafter. They will forever be erased from everyone's memories as if they never existed. Unfortunately for them it may be a hellish eternity.

Once again, we will not enter heaven by our good works and good deeds but only by our belief and acceptance in the Lord as our savior.

II Timothy 4:8 (NIV)

[I have kept the faith]Now there is in store for me the crown of righteousness, which the Lord, the righteous Judge, will award to me on that day -- and not only to me, but also to all who have longed for his appearing.

Tomorrow is promised to no one!

Angels

It doesn't seem possible to discuss heaven without at least mentioning angels.

As a child growing up in the United States, I thought everyone believed, as I did, that we all magically go to heaven and become angels when we die. Wasn't this a popular belief in the 1940s and 1950s? Or maybe it was just in my neighborhood. I never gave it a second thought until one day more than fifty years later when I realized we are God's children and not his angels which meant we would never claim a pair of wings! We would never fly!

In the Bible we are told God made his heavens at the same time he made the earth, the entire universe and everything within.

> ***Genesis 1:1 (KJV)***
> *In the beginning God created the heaven and the earth.*
> ***Genesis 2:1 (ASV)***
> *And the heavens and the earth were finished [created], and all the host of [everything within] them.*

So the heavens in all their glory, where God and his countless thousands of angels, cherubim and heavenly beings abide, were formed.

Various angelic beings of opalescent radiance are sometimes described as ministering spirits consisting of light, fire and breath. They are the Lord's servants; the Lord's messengers who execute his commands and who are mighty (in number and size) fearless warriors. Although it seems unlikely there are guardian angels *per se*, on occasion

God appoints to specific believers, angels for protection and guidance.

> **Psalm 91:11**
>
> *For he [God] will give his angels charge over you, to [guard you and] keep you in all your ways;*

The Bible tells us of angels who have thoughts and feelings, who make decisions and are curious. Under the care of Christ and the Holy Spirit, angels attend to waiting saints (God's devoted people) or heirs by protecting them, by opposing powers of evil spirits, and by comforting and instructing their souls.

> **Luke 22:43 (KJV)**
>
> *... there appeared an angel unto him [Jesus] from heaven, strengthening him*

Archangels are thought to be the highest ranking angels. One mentioned by name in the original (King James Version) Bible translation is the mighty archangel Michael. Gabriel is referred to in the books of Daniel and Luke. Catholic Bibles include some books (not found in protestant testaments) which name both Gabriel and Raphael as archangels also. In the Book of Tobit (not included in our protestant Bible today) archangel Raphael identifies himself as one of the seven trumpeted angels referred to in the Book of Revelation. Surely, all seven must be archangels.

> **Revelation 8:2 (KJV)**
>
> *And I saw the seven angels which stood before God; and to them were given seven trumpets.*

Also in the Book of Tobit, we are told how Raphael returned Tobit's sight, and saved his life and that of his son Tobias. In the Book of Enoch, Raphael is also a major figure. The Coptic Church recognizes the archangel of salvation Uriel, even though the Catholic Church no longer officially recognizes him.

Other ancient texts name other archangels as well, all of whom are God's holy messengers. So, how many archangels are there? Some say twelve, some say thousands. God only knows.

Catholic tradition suggests all heavenly hosts are organized into an hierarchy of levels and divisions called choirs. Besides Archangels there are angels without wings, there are the winged cherubim and Seraphim and there are Thrones, and Ophanim. Others are Dominions, Virtues, Powers and Authorities. These celestial beings appear to collaborate with each other and with Principalities.

One other angel mentioned is Lucifer...perhaps better known as Satan or the devil. It is written that about one-third of God's angels followed Lucifer in his quest for supremacy.

II Peter 2:4

For God did not have pity on or spare the angels that sinned. He had them tied up in chains and thrown into hell's pits of darkness, until the time of judgment.

Jude 1:6

And the angels who kept not their positions of authority [own domain], but abandoned their own proper home, God has kept in darkness and in everlasting chains until the day of the great judgment.

Chapter 2

The Alternative

Mark 12:24
*And answering, Jesus said to them,
Isn't this where you make your mistake
and go wrong, because you don't know
either the Scriptures or the power of
God.*

It was about thirty years ago when I was nine months
pregnant with my youngest son that I received that well-
known dreaded telephone call saying that my father had died
unexpectedly. It was his heart. As I recall, my Caesarian
Section was postponed only a week while I went home to
help mother make the final arrangements.

Just a few months previously Dad had mentioned
to me that he knew for sure *how* he was going to die. It
was a strange comment coming from him since death was
a topic our family rarely discussed. Upon my pestering
him relentlessly, he later admitted experiencing the most
unforgettable, realistic dream in which he had died in a car
accident. He was absolutely convinced he knew his fate!

Now dad was a nice guy with a big heart, intelligent
and a super great story teller who most everybody couldn't
help but love. With a little encouragement and respect, I
think he might have been successful in life. Perhaps it's safe
to say he lived on the fringe. He never attended church but
he often visited the racetracks and Las Vegas. As a child, I
remember his best friend was a bookie.

Once, after another friend dragged him to a Billy Graham event, I remember him questioning much about life itself. For a long time he seemed to be searching for answers but now, looking back on it, I realize he didn't know where to find his answers; or perhaps even to know the right questions to ask. One day he steadfastly announced that "when you die, you're dead" and "this is all there is." "Life here on earth is either our heaven or hell".

Gratefully, dad didn't die in an ugly car accident. He had just taken a shower when he had his fatal heart attack. It was about a week or two later when I had my unforgettable dream. You know the kind that wakes you up so you can't get back to sleep. The kind that makes you wake up someone else to share the experience with. The kind that is so real to life that you're sure it wasn't a dream at all.

My dream started with my dad telephoning me. As we began small-talking I was gradually able to see him on the other end of the phone line. It was as if I was watching him on a movie screen or through a huge window. From a drab cheap-looking motel room he said he was calling me to see if I was alright. I carefully scanned the room as we continued to talk. He didn't want me to be concerned about him. He said he was OK. He said he was just waiting. I said how in the world are you managing there without a television; or worse yet, your cigarettes. Two things he couldn't live without for very long. Then, as I came into an understanding awareness, I told him he could put down the telephone. He hesitated until I convinced him I understood. He told me he thought using the phone (as a prop) would be less shocking, less traumatic for me.

Much too soon our chat was over. Dad admitted he wasn't staying in that motel room. He didn't know where he was. He didn't know how long before he was to move on. It was all for my benefit he said. He didn't know how to explain anything other than he was waiting.

When the memory and impact of a dream more than thirty years ago still seems like it was only yesterday, then perhaps it had a meaning, or a purpose. It certainly was very powerful.

Satan

Satan too, believes in God's existence although we certainly cannot consider him a *Believer*. Satan, known by many different names is not easily recognizable because of his many disguises. Usually called the devil, the enemy, the serpent or the dragon, he is sometimes referred to as Lucifer, the Prince of Darkness, or the Prince of demons, the adversary, the deceiver as well as others.

An August 2002 poll by Barna Research showed that:

- Most American adults (59%) consider that Satan is simply a symbol or concept or principle of evil, not an actual personality.

- Three in four Roman Catholics believe this; 55% of Protestants agree.

- A minority of adults (34%) believe Satan to be a living being with supernatural powers.

We all know that Satan is not the traditional red-suited long-tailed character with a goatee, horns and pitchfork. He was a beautiful and powerful (magnificent) angel who was known as Lucifer, the son of the morning. Perhaps he was even an archangel but is often described, as a cherubim guarding the holiest ark of the covenant. In any case, his sinful pride (and also perhaps envy) motivated his determination to surmount God by deceiving one-third of the angels into supporting his battle for the throne.

Revelation 12:7, (ASV)

*And there was war in heaven: Michael
and his angels going forth to war with
the dragon and the dragon warred and
his angels*

*12:8 And they prevailed not, neither
was their place found any more in
heaven.*

*12:9 And the great dragon was cast
down, the old serpent, he that is called
the Devil and Satan, the deceiver of the
whole world; he was cast down to the
earth, and his angels were cast down
with him.*

Satan is a profoundly evil, fallen angel (rebel angel)
who is totally dedicated to the destruction of everyone's
lives. He is a spirit being: a supernatural thief who comes
only to steal, kill and destroy. Satan and his demons (aka
unclean spirits) are all-pervasive. They are a continual threat
to most everyone because of their never-ceasing endeavors
to engage in world-wide spiritual warfare. Their efforts are
focused on making us believe that everlasting life is not a
reality: On convincing us this world is all there is. Once
they successfully attack the soul, they can easily attack the
body.

John 10:10 (ASV)

*The thief cometh not, but that he may
steal, and kill, and destroy: I came that
they may have life, and may have it
abundantly.*

John 10:10

[again, a widely-used familiar version]
The thief (devil) comes only to steal,
kill and destroy. But I (Jesus) came that
you might have and enjoy your life in
abundance, to the full, until it over-
flows.

My only experience (possibly) with evil spirits was a brief encounter early one morning at a relative's house when they were out of town and I was house sitting. I was awakened just after daybreak, to find two men standing at the foot of my bed. Although one was slightly taller than the other, both were middle aged with dark hair and each was wearing a different plaid red shirt.

As I sat up frightened, I realized both men were standing at the end of the bed, on the other side of the bed's footboard. But that was impossible because a settee was there at the end of the bed. Slowly, both men slithered backwards in unison. With each step they took backwards, they increasingly faded into thin air. Poof! Gone.

Since that time a few years ago, I have given this strange, unbelievable sighting very much thought. No, I really do not know what to make of it. I do know that I was awake, it was daylight and that it did happen as I told you here.

The only clue or lead I have is a tiny, nagging thought I had at the time it was happening that these silly men were trying to make me think they were someone else; someone I knew who had passed away long before. Someone they were trying to emulate who had darkhair and often wore a red patterned shirt. That is how I remember him. But their shapes and sizes were wrong and the patterns on the red shirts were wrong. But since I have never verbalized any specific details, and neither Satan nor his demons can read my mind, they were unable to impersonate this person accurately.

Although powerful, Satan is unable to become victorious because he cannot give life, he cannot heal anyone and he cannot read our thoughts. Above all, God has given us power and authority over Satan. We must remember we have authority to "rebuke" evil and its actions. We have ability to "bind" evil and curtail its activities. We need not fear Satan or his evil spirits (demons).

A recent Gallop poll states:
30% of all Christians in the United States don't believe evil spirits exist.

Revelation 12:10 exposes the devil as the "accuser of our brethren" who accuses us before God day and night. But the good news is that we don't have to worry about his accusations. In fact, he seldom has any dealings with righteous people because he knows he cannot corrupt us.

Fear is the opposite of faith. The more fearful we become, the less faithful we are which also means the more faithful we become, the less fearful we are. The amount of fear we tolerate is inversely related to the amount of faith we affirm. Where along this continuum are you?

Fearful_____|_____**Faithful**

Fear contaminates faith. Fear is unbelief. We must not fear because Satan (evil) creeps into our lives. If we become fearful or doubtful, then it is often expressed by anger.

I Peter 5:8 (NIV)

Be self-controlled and alert. Your enemy the devil prowls around like a roaring lion looking for someone to devour.

I Peter 5:8 Again,

Be well balanced (temperate, sober of mind) be vigilant and cautious at all times; for that enemy of yours, the devil, roams around like a lion roaring [in fierce hunger], seeking someone to seize upon and devour.

Gospel authors wrote of exorcisms which drove out demons who afflicted people. Over the years there have been many recorded instances of demon possession where Satan and/or his demons have been thought to dwell within us.

Luke 4:35 (ASV)

And Jesus rebuked him [the foul spirit of a demon], saying, Hold thy peace, and come out of him. And when the demon had thrown him [the man] down [onto the floor] in the midst, he came out of him, having done him no hurt.

Acts 16:16,

As we were going down to the place of prayer, we were met by a demon possessed slave girl. She claimed to foretell the future and know of secret events; thereby earning a great deal of money for her masters.

16:17 She kept following Paul and the rest of us, shouting loudly, "These men are servants of the Most High God, and they have come to tell you how to find salvation."

16:18 And she did this day after day until Paul got so annoyed that he finally turned and said to the demon within her, "I command you in the name of Jesus Christ to come out of her" And at that verymoment it left her.

Hell and Hades

In 1983 eighty six percent of the American people said they believed there is a hell. Twenty five years later, the numbers are barely in the double digits. What has happened to our spiritual knowledge. And is it the fault of our families or our churches?

Souls are said to pass into hell by God's irrevocable declaration usually at the eventual throne of judgment but in some cases immediately after death. This condemnation is the logical result when our soul uses its free will, endowed by God, to reject the will of God. This is God's justice in action because God will not interfere with our soul's freedom of choice. We are responsible for the choices we make.

Hell is not a punishment from God
but a self-condemnation

Hell is the separation from God and His presence. It is the zip code of the devil Satan and the forces of evil (although their spirits roam the earth). Commonly, hell is a holding place until the final judgment is declared. The great gulf of hell was created for Satan and his angels. There is no way out of hell's bitter darkness and unrelenting torment.

The realm of the dead is biblically described as divided into two halves by a great gulf (hell). On one side of the schism is paradise and the other, Hades. A place of regret, death and separation from God.

II Peter 2:4 (KJV)
For if God spared not the angels that sinned, but cast them down to hell, and

delivered them into chains of darkness,
to be reserved unto judgment;

This is the belief of most protestant traditions. Hell, sometimes referred to as Hades, is a place created by God for the punishment of the devil and his followers of fallen angels and other wicked souls. Yes, so-called good people will end up in hades even though they love, because they love things, or themselves but not God.

The gospel of Luke tells us about a rich man who repeatedly ignored helping a sickly beggar named Lazarus. After they both died, they found themselves on opposite sides of a great, impenetrable schism between paradise and hell.

> ### *Luke 16:23, (KJV)*
> *And in hell he lift up his eyes, being in torments, and saw Abraham afar off [across a great gulf], and Lazarus in his bosom.*
>
> *16:26 And...between us and you there is a great gulf fixed, that they which would pass from hence to you may not be able, and that none may cross over from thence to us.*

The Lake of Fire

The lake of fire (and brimstone) is the second death. It is the final death. It is the eternal death. But it is not really a death at all but rather an eternal damnation. As spiritual souls who exist beyond the loss of our physical earthly bodies, it is up to us whether or not we choose eternal life. If not, we are left with no other alternative.

Revelation 21:8 (ASV)

But for the fearful, and unbelieving, and abominable, and murderers, and fornicators, and sorcerers, and idolaters, and all liars, their part shall be in the lake that burns with fire and brimstone [sulfur]: which is the second death.

Revelation 20:13, (KJV)

And the sea gave up the dead that were in it; and death and hell [Hades] gave up the dead that were in them: and they were judged every man according to their works.

20:14 *Then death and Hades were cast [thrown] into the lake of fire. The lake of fire is the second death.*

Revelation 20:10 (KJV)

And the devil that deceived them was cast into the lake of fire and brimstone, where the beast and the false prophet are, and shall be tormented day and night for ever and ever.

If we die without asking forgiveness and accepting God's merciful love we are damned to remain separated from Him forever by our own free choice. Not only will we be excluded from his presence forever, but we will have continual and eternal memory of our mistakes together with sorrowful regret: eternal damnation.

Mark 16:16 (ASV)

He that believes and is baptized shall be saved; but he that disbelieves shall be condemned.

Matthew 25:41 (ASV)

Then shall he say also unto them on the left hand, Depart from me, ye cursed, into the [everlasting] eternal fire which is prepared for the devil and his angels:

Revelation 20:15 (KJV)

And whosoever was not found written in the book of life was cast into the lake of fire.

The lake of fire and brimstone is where sinners will be committed after the judgment and where they will suffer punishment. There will be no turning back, changing your mind or no other chance. It has been described as a solitary emptiness. A darkness where you will be totally alone forever.

Theatrically it has been portrayed as concealed behind massive gates which muffle the crying and wailing of multitudes.Bodies resembling earthly forms are eternally tormented with fire consuming their flesh but since they are without blood or life itself, they cannot die.

Chapter 3

Judgment

II Corinthians 5:10 (NLT)
For we must all stand before Christ to be judged. We will each receive whatever we deserve for the good or evil we have done in this earthly body.

A Psalm of David tells us that Jehovah (a name for God in Hebrew scripture) will judge the world in righteousness by fairly administering judgment to his people. Second Corinthians informs us that we all must appear before the judgment seat of Christ to be revealed. The Lord will compensate us according to our works and achievements (whether good or evil) and take into consideration our motives, purposes and diligence. For the Lord sees our hearts.

Psalm 9:7 (KJV)
But the LORD shall endure for ever: he hath prepared his throne for judgment.

God will not judge us but has entrusted all judgment to the Son, Jesus.

John 5:21, (ASV)
For as the Father raises the dead and giveth them life, even so the Son also giveth life to whom he will.

5:22 For neither does the Father judge any man, but he has given all judgment unto the Son;

5:23 that all may honor the Son, even as they honor the Father. He that honors not the Son honors not the Father that sent him.

A *Believer* does not merely accept the Lord but obeys and surrenders unto Him. The new testament explains that *Believers*, although perhaps present at the throne of judgment, are not judged but pass directly into eternal life. Their names are forever inscribed in the (Lamb's) book of life.

*John 5:24 (ASV)

Verily, verily, I say unto you, He that hears my word, and believes him that sent me, has eternal life and comes not into judgment but has passed out of death into [eternal] life

Exodus 32:33 (KJV)

And the LORD said unto Moses, Whosoever has sinned against me, him will I blot out of my book.

I often use the term *Believers* (aka followers) herein to mean those who actively follow Christ and believe with their hearts (also referred to as born-again Christians) as opposed to those who believe with their heads. For Satan is a prime example of one who believes and knows the existence of Christ but certainly is not a *Believer*!

Revelation 20:12, 15 (KJV)

And I saw the dead, small and great, stand before God; and the books were opened: and another book was opened, which is the book of life: and the dead were judged out of those things which were written in the books, according to their works.

20:15 And whosoever was not found written in the book of life was cast into the lake of fire.

Daniel 7:10 (ASV)

A fiery stream issued and came forth from before him: thousands of thousands ministered unto him, and ten thousand times ten thousand stood before him: the judgment was set, and the books were opened.

John 5:29 (ASV)

And shall come forth; they that have done good, unto the resurrection of life; and they that have done evil, unto the resurrection of judgment.

Jeremiah 1:16

"I will pronounce My judgments on them concerning all their wickedness, whereby they have forsaken Me and have offered sacrifices to other gods, and worshiped the works of their own hands.

James 2:13 (NLT)

There will be no mercy for those who have not shown mercy to others. But if you have been merciful, God will be merciful when he judges you.

I John 4:17 (NLT)

And as we live in God our love grows more perfect. So we will not be afraid on the day of judgment, but we can face him with confidence; because we live like Jesus here in this world.

In Revelation, the last book of the New Testament, the Apostle John describes his vision of the judgment at the Great White Throne.

Revelation 20:11,

I saw a great white throne with some-one sitting on it. Earth and heaven tried to run away, but there was no place for them to go.

20:12 I also saw all the dead people standing in front of that throne. Every one of them was there, no matter who they had once been. Several books were opened, and then the book of life was opened. The dead were judged by what those books said they had done.

20:13 The sea gave up the dead people who were in it, and death and its kingdom also gave up their dead. Then everyone was judged by what they had done.

20:14 Afterwards, death and its kingdom were thrown into the lake of fire. This is the second death.

Matthew 25:41

Then He shall say to those on [His] left hand, "Depart from Me, you cursed ones into the eternal [everlasting] fire which has been prepared for the devil and his angels.

Matthew 25:46 (NIV)

Then they will go away to eternal [everlasting] punishment, but the righteous to eternal life.

The Lord speaks in Isaiah 66 how he will choose the most dreaded punishments if you are turning away from him while choosing your own pleasures and delights. In so doing you are evil; not listening to or answering God's call. Romans 2 tells us that if you are stubborn and refuse to accept God you are only making things worse for yourself because you will experience God's wrath on judgment day.

Matthew 12:36,

I tell you that on the day of judgment, we will give an accounting for every idle, careless word we speak.

12:37 By your words you will be justified [acquitted], and by your words you will be condemned [and sentenced].

God has given us a free will to make our own decisions. We know that smart decisions are usually arrived at when we know everything we can about a subject from more than one point of view. And for the things we can't know for sure, a little faith may be our salvation.

Once again, eternal damnation is a choice we make rather than a punishment God hands down.

John 12:48

Anyone who rejects me and rejects my words and teachings has one who judges him: for the word [message] that I have spoken will itself judge and convict him in the last day.

John 9:39 (NLT)

Then Jesus told him, "I entered this world to render judgment -- [as a Separator, in order that there may be separation between those who believe on Me and those who reject Me] to give sight to the blind and to show those who think they see that they are blind"

*John 3:3 (KJV)

Jesus answered and said unto him [Nicodemus], Verily, verily, I say unto thee, Except a man be born again, he cannot see the kingdom of God.

Epilogue

Proverbs 22:4 (KJV)

By humility and the fear [respectful reverence] of the LORD are riches, and honor, and [long] life.

Again, when we put God first in everything we do, He puts us first in everything He does. Seek first God and the world will come to you. Seek first the kingdom of God and all things will be added to you.

*John 3:16 (KJV)

For God so loved the world, that he gave his only begotten Son, that whosoever believeth in him should not perish, but have everlasting life.

According to God's word, in order to have everlasting life, we need only to believe in Him. That does not mean to simply believe that Jesus lived two thousand years ago. But rather that he is our living God who wants to become an associate in our day-to-day lives. He is the Son of our supernatural, perfect God who is the omnipotent (unlimited in power and authority), omniscient (all-knowing) originator and ruler of the universe. Omnipotent, omnipresent, and omniscient, meaning all mighty power being everywhere present at the same time.

II Peter 1:2 (NLT)

May God give you more and more grace and peace as you grow in your knowledge of God and Jesus our Lord.

Ephesians 3:17 (NLT)
Then Christ will make his home in
your hearts as you trust in him. Your
roots will grow down into God's love
and keep you strong.

As Americans living in the freedom of the United States it is easy for some of us to forget that freedom does not give us a license to do anything we want but rather is a privilege God gives to us to always do the right thing! God's love, compassion and His mercy are new every morning of every day. Each new day is filled with hope and possibilities. God is interested in which paths we will walk during this lifetime because they will lead us to His plans and purpose for our lives and for our future.

Acts 20:24 (NLT)
But my life is worth nothing to me un-
less I use it for finishing the work as-
signed me by the Lord Jesus—the work
of telling others the Good News about
the wonderful grace of God.
I Timothy 4:12 (KJV)
...be thou an example of the believers,
in word, in conversation, in charity, in
spirit, in faith, in purity.

I heard a stunning statistic recently on television. In the United States, the divorce rate (which is now about fifty percent) was compared to the divorce rate for couples who pray together, which is only one divorce in every ten thousand marriages! Wow! Wouldn't you think anyone contemplating a lasting marriage would seriously give this some thought? Obviously, couples who pray together stay together. Stay in faith, release your faith and reach out to others in need.

Romans 15:33 (NLT)
And now, may God who gives us his peace, be with you all. Amen.

Special Prayers

What is it they say about the earnest prayer of a righteous person? As I recall, that kind of prayer has great power and produces wonderful results. Included are some favorite verses, words and affirmations I have found helpful. Some are especially effective when repeated frequently.

A new day:

Psalm 118:24 (KJV)
This is the day which the Lord has made; we will rejoice and be glad in it.

Philippians 4:13 (KJV)
I can do all things through Christ which strengthens me.

Hebrews 13:5 (NIV)
...God has said, Never will I leave you; Never will I forsake you.

Matthew 6:34 (NLT)
So don't worry about tomorrow, for tomorrow will bring its own worries. Today's trouble is enough for today.

Blessings and Promises:

- *He is the rewarder of those who diligently seek Him.*

- *If God be for me, who can be against me?*

- *If we cast our cares on God, He works in our behalf.*

- *Accept blindly and say, God, I trust you, it's not up to me.*

- *Angels are prospering me right now*

- *To whom much is given, much is required.*

- *Release blessings by saying out loud "I bless _____ "*

- *All things are possible with God.*

Psalm 37:4 (KJV)
Delight thyself also in the Lord; and he shall give thee the desires of thine heart.

Psalm 55:22 (KJV)
Cast your burden upon the LORD, and he shall sustain thee.

John 15:7 (KJV)
If ye abide in me, and my words abide in you, ye shall ask what ye will, and it shall be done unto you.

Matthew 6:25 (NIV)
Therefore I tell you, do not worry about your life, what you will eat or drink; or about your body, what you will wear. Is not life more important than food, and the body more important than clothes?

Philippians 4:19 (ASV)
And my God shall supply every need of yours according to his riches in glory in Christ Jesus.

Thankfulness:

I Thessalonians 5:18 (KJV)
In every thing give thanks: for this is the will of God in Christ Jesus concerning you.

Ephesians 5:20 (NIV)
always giving thanks to God the Father for everything, in the name of our Lord Jesus Christ.

Fear:

II Timothy 1:7 (KJV)
For God hath not given us the spirit of fear; but of power, and of love, and of a sound mind.

John 14:27 (ASV)
Peace I leave with you, my peace I give unto you: not as the world giveth, give I unto you. Let not your heart be troubled, neither let it be afraid.

~"Get thee behind me, Satan"
~"I command _____ in the name of Jesus Christ."

Healing:

~ The healing power of God is working in me right now and every minute of every day.

~Every day I get better and better in everyway.

~ I Believe that I have received; I am healed and made whole.

Moving forward:

Proverbs 3:5, (KJV)

Trust in the LORD with all thine heart; and lean not unto thine own understanding.

3:6 In all thy ways acknowledge him, and he shall direct thy paths.

Romans 8:28 (KJV)

And we know that all things work together for good to them that love God, to them who are the called according to his purpose.

I John 1:9 (KJV)

If we confess our sins, he is faithful and just to forgive us our sins, and to cleanse us from all unrighteousness.

***Romans 10:13 (ASV)**

for, Whosoever shall call upon the name of the Lord shall be saved.

The Lord is good and his mercy endures forever.

God Bless You,
God Bless America!